INTRODUCTION

Starting a small business can be a great and rewarding undertaking, provided you are equipped with the proper tools. This book will help you discover those tools, and will direct you to the many services and opportunities available to you.

The Ministry of Industry, Trade and Technology offers many programs for small firms such as financial planning, management methods, marketing, technological innovation - even how to sell your product and services to all levels of government.

There are 26 Business Self-Help offices and 18 ministry offices throughout Ontario, each with a staff committed to serving community interests. Their job is to help you. For a full listing of offices, see page 110.

Take advantage of the ministry's expertise and assistance to develop a business which will contribute to your own growth and prosperity and to the future of Ontario.

Many textbooks have been written on the operation of small businesses. These are available through public libraries and bookstores, and it is not the purpose of this publication to duplicate or attempt to summarize what has already been done.

Instead, we hope to make prospective business people aware of the base requirements, and assist them in evaluating both themselves and the business being contemplated.

In short, this is not a "how to" book, but concentrates rather on "what to do" before making any investment of time or money.

It also stresses that the dominant factors required for the success of any business are dedication, experience, adequate financing and hard work.

The information in the publication is current at the time of printing, to the best of our knowledge.

Ontario

| Minister of Industry, Trade and Technology | Le ministre de l'Industrie, du Commerce et de la Technologie | Hearst Block Queen's Park Toronto, Ontario M7A 2E1 416/965-1617 | Èdifice Hearst Queen's Park Toronto (Ontario) M7A 2E1 416/965-1617 |

I am pleased to introduce this nineteenth edition of "Starting a Small Business in Ontario" and to welcome IBM Canada Ltd. as a co-sponsor in its publication.

The important contribution of small businesses to our economy cannot be overstated. From the development of innovative technology, to the introduction of new services and the creation of new employment opportunities for Ontarians, entrepreneurship benefits us all.

At the heart of every new business is an entrepreneur with confidence in his or her business idea and a willingness to accept the hard work and long hours necessary for success. Ontario's entrepreneurs represent a broad cross-section of men and women, like you, who start and operate businesses to manufacture products and to provide services and retail goods.

This book will help you plan the start-up of your business. As well, Ministry staff, through our network of Business Self-Help Offices, are available to assist you in discovering the services and opportunities available.

On behalf of my Ministry, I am proud to welcome you as a new entrepreneur in Ontario and to wish you every success in your new business enterprise.

Sincerely,

Allan C. Pilkey
Minister
Industry, Trade and Technology

IBM

IBM Canada Ltd.

251 Consumers Road
North York, Ontario
M2J 4R3
(416) 758-3311

IBM Canada Ltd. is pleased to again be working in partnership with the Ministry of Industry, Trade and Technology to co-sponsor the publication of "Starting a Small Business in Ontario". We believe that this booklet can be of invaluable assistance to anyone seeking practical advice on setting up their own company.

The development of small business is extremely important to Ontario's economic health. During the 1980's, for example, more than 80 percent of new job creation came from this sector.

Small business is important to IBM Canada as well. We depend on smaller firms to provide us with a variety of activities crucial to the operation of our business, including retail sales, software development and product components.

Most visible among these are our IBM Business Partners, who help us market many of our information handling products and services. In most cases these companies and firms would not have come into existence had it not been for the efforts of individual Canadian entrepreneurs. We would like to think that this publication will encourage others to follow in their footsteps.

We at IBM believe so strongly in the importance of small business that we've developed a unit that's fully dedicated to meeting the sector's special needs and requirements. This organization has worked with literally hundreds of new companies over the years, so please feel free to draw on our experience and expertise.

In the meantime, best wishes—and good luck!

Sincerely,

Barry Goode

J.C. Barry Goode
Marketing Operations Manager
Small Business

Cable: INBUSMACH
Telex: 06-966574

ACKNOWLEDGMENTS

In the preparation of this book, we have drawn on many sources of information. These include other ministries of both the provincial and the federal government; banks and other financial institutions; various business textbooks; publications of the Small Business Administration (Washington, D.C.); and many other sources.

These other sources are credited in the section in which the information appears. We also wish to thank A.E. LePage Commercial Real Estate Services, Toronto, for its guidance in the preparation of the information on leasing of retail, commercial and industrial space, and how to own your own office space; and the Insurance Bureau of Canada for its assistance in the preparation of the information on surety bonds.

CONTENTS

CHAPTER 1 :
THE ENTREPRENEUR

So you want to be an "entrepreneur"! You have made a

very important decision, but have you really considered all

the implications?

THE PERSON

Almost everyone has thought about starting a business at some point: the independence it would bring; the thought of being your own boss; the opportunity to earn profits; the idea of being a decision maker; and the freedom from routine. All these are powerful motivating factors. But the decision to enter into business cannot be solely based on emotion. The decision will affect your personal life in many ways, some of which this book will discuss in detail.

To be an entrepreneur is to be a risk taker. At the heart of every new business is an entrepreneur; someone not content to leave things as they are, but wanting to strike out on his or her own. This individual brings two important ingredients to the new business: confidence in an idea and a willingness to accept the hard work and long hours necessary for success.

Confidence and hard work are starting points, but there are other considerations:

- the need for your product or service;
- a self-evaluation of your preparedness;
- a basic understanding of the business you are entering;
- the development of a business plan; and, most importantly,
- money.

All of these aspects of starting and operating a business will be important to the success of your idea. Some must be attended to at the outset, others will become more important as you proceed, but all of them will require your attention sooner or later.

The decision to enter business and the choice of which business to enter must be your own. Before you set the wheels in motion, it is important for you to evaluate your motivation and capabilities.

Prior to opening this book, you will have considered the possibilities for:

- personal satisfaction;
- the accumulation of wealth;
- independence.

A successful business can offer you all of these, but ask yourself:

- Why do I want to be in business? Am I confident I can succeed?
- Do I have any experience in my choice of business and if not, how do I obtain it?
- Am I a risk taker? Do I understand the implications of my decision?
- Should I maintain my current employment or will my business provide an adequate income by itself?
- Is my family supportive and understanding?

Being your own boss can offer great personal satisfaction, but with it comes the responsibility for making and living with your decisions. The right decision offers profit and success. The wrong decision can cost you money. Too many wrong decisions can put you out of business. Your decision to enter business will have implications for your lifestyle. Operating a business will affect your privacy, friendships and security, as well as your financial status.

Now that you've considered some of the personal implications of starting your own business, you must assess your financial position. The following chart will help you in this regard. It should become part of the business plan you develop before making that final decision to go into business.

To assist you in this, and in the following sections of the book, a glossary of business and financial terms is included at the end of Chapter 1.

PERSONAL STATEMENT OF AFFAIRS
AND GENERAL INFORMATION

NAME: _____ DATE: _____

ADDRESS: _____

PHONE: HOME _____ BUSINESS _____ AGE: _____ DEPENDENTS: _____
( ) ( )

PRESENT EMPLOYMENT: _____ HOW LONG WITH
THIS EMPLOYER:

PREVIOUS EMPLOYER _____ HOW LONG: _____

SALARY, WAGES OR COMMISSION   OTHER INCOME   SOURCE:
PER ANNUM: PER ANNUM:
$ _____ $ _____

GUARANTEES ON DEBTS OF OTHERS: AMOUNT
NAME

ASSETS

BANK ACCOUNTS	☐
STOCKS AT COST	(Market Value): $ ☐
BONDS AT COST	(Market Value): $ ☐
LIFE INSURANCE C.S.V.	Beneficiary: ☐
AUTOMOBILE	Year: Make: ☐
HOME	Registered: Building Size: Lot Size: ☐
OTHER ASSETS	☐
TOTAL	☐

LIABILITIES

BANK LOAN	☐
RENT	☐
CHARGE ACCOUNTS	☐
LOANS	☐
UTILITIES	☐
FOOD/CLOTHING	☐
INSTALLMENT PURCHASES	☐
MORTGAGES	Interest Rate: Term: Payments: ☐
TAXES	☐
OTHER LIABILITIES	☐
SUB TOTAL	☐

NET WORTH   TOTAL   ☐

3

Being in business brings with it not only rewards but also inherent risks and pitfalls. At the earliest stages of development it is particularly important to minimize the risks in order to maximize the rewards. Two factors can help tip the scale in a positive direction: development of good business management skills and a well-thought-out business plan with a sense of direction and a yardstick for success.

Management

Management means much more than giving orders. It involves the maximum utilization of money, people and other resources to achieve the desired result. It also involves keeping and interpreting records to evaluate changes, trends and weaknesses.

According to Dun & Bradstreet, the largest single cause of business failure in Canada is poor management. If you are the owner or partner in a small business, its success or failure will depend on your management skills. Those skills will be tested even before the business is established.

Experience is the greatest of all teachers. Through it, you learn to avoid mistakes and anticipate the consequences of any given action, plan alternatives, gauge your resources and profit from advantages. If you have no experience in the type of business that you propose to start (or a similar business), you would be well advised to work for a while for someone else who is already established.

You must have confidence in yourself. Confident people take the initiative - people who take the initiative are decision-makers and decisions are pivotal in business.

If your confidence is based on knowledge and experience, you are much more likely to be successful.

Going into business always involves some risk. You can reduce that risk factor by careful planning. Your chance of success will depend to a very large extent on how well you have examined all aspects of the operation you are proposing to start.

4

Hard work and a marketable product or service are important to a business - but they aren't enough. In order to succeed, you need to establish detailed, obtainable objectives and goals plus definite time limits for reaching them.

To help you make these vital decisions - and to aid potential advisors in your business in understanding them clearly - it is important for you to prepare a business plan. This will enable you to be forewarned of any problems you might encounter in the future and, at the same time, you'll be prepared to take advantage of opportunities when they come your way.

The Business Plan

The business plan is a written summary of the overall activities of your enterprise. It is a report on the company's sources and use of funds, management personnel, labour relations, products, marketing strategy, production techniques and research. It describes the past, present and future of your operation.

A typical business plan begins with a summary of your idea, the market need, the amount of capital required and the projected financial results expressed as a rate of return. Follow this with a table of contents and then the plan itself.

The first component should describe the background of the business and a brief outline of the basic operation. It's necessary as well to include information about how your company is organized and who is involved, in order to establish that management is capable of carrying out the plan.

Follow this with your plans for marketing, which must convince the reader that your company has a product, process or service that is different and worthy of support.

The final component is financial; here you should explain your projected income and expenses month by month.

Other Resources

The Ministry of Industry, Trade and Technology has prepared several workbooks for the service, retail and manufacturing sectors which you may find useful as you plan your business. Each workbook covers theory, examples of putting the theory into practice and blank forms for your use. Topics include: How to Prepare a Business Plan, which enlarges on the information given here; and Marketing, which illustrates the importance of marketing and how to develop a marketing plan for your business.

These publications are available for a modest fee from your local Business Self-Help office (see page 110 for locations) or from Publications Ontario. To order by mail or telephone, use the tear-out mail order card.

GLOSSARY OF BUSINESS TERMS*

accountant
one who is skilled at keeping business records. Usually, the name "accountant" refers to a highly trained professional rather than one who keeps books.

account
a record of a business transaction or "deal". When you buy something on credit, the company you are dealing with sets up an "account". This means it sets up a record of what you buy and what you pay. You will do the same thing with any customers to whom you extend credit.

accounts receivable
a record of what is owed to you. All of the credit "accounts" - the record of what each customer owes you - taken together are your "accounts receivable".

analysis
breaking an idea or a problem down into its parts or a good examination of the parts of anything. In business you must "analyze" that is make an "analysis" of, a problem before you can decide on the best solution. Let's say that your problem is some item that isn't selling well. You "make an analysis" by gathering all the facts as to why the item is not selling.

asset
anything of worth that is owned. Your personal assets (not counting your abilities) are the money you have in your pocket or in the bank, whatever is owed to you, any securities that you own, the property you own, whatever part of your home that you own, your furniture and appliances and all the miscellaneous things that you personally own. The assets of a business are just the same: money in the bank, accounts receivable, securities held in the name of the business, property or buildings, equipment, fixtures, merchandise for sale or being made ready, supplies and all things of value that the business owns.

---

*Reproduced with permission of the United States Federal Small Business Administration, Washington. (Revised to reflect the Canadian context.)

articles of incorporation

a legal document filed with the province and / or federally that sets forth the purposes and regulations for a corporation. These papers must be approved by the province and/or federally before a corporation legally exists and is allowed to do business.

bad debts

money owed to you that you can't collect. A business should never give credit or loan money to anyone who is not a good risk. But you can't be positive you are going to collect everything from those to whom you do give credit or money.

balance

the amount of money remaining in an account. The total of your money in the bank after accounting for all transactions (deposits and withdrawals) is called a "balance".

balance sheet

an important business document that shows what a business owns and owes as of the date shown. Essentially a "balance sheet" is a list of business assets and their cost on one side and a list of liabilities and owners' equity (investment in the business) on the other side with the amount for each. The liabilities include all that the business owes.

bookkeeping

the process of recording business transactions in the accounting records. It is very important to keep accurate and complete financial records and a good bookkeeping system will be a great help.

break-even point

where the income is equal to the outgo. The level of business at which the revenue (income) exactly equals the expenses (outgo).

budget

a plan expressed in money terms. How much money do you need to run the business? How much money do you think will be coming in?

capital
available money to invest or the total of accumulated assets available for production. Put another way, your capital for going into business is the total of your property and money resources that you can make available for the business and whatever you will need to live on while getting the business going.

capital requirement
a list (or schedule) of expenses that must be met to establish a business. Even before a business is started, the owner should start keeping records.

cash
money in hand or readily available. Currency - hard money, bills and negotiable securities (like checks) - in your cash drawer is cash. But so is the money you can draw on demand - your bank accounts or savings accounts also represent "cash". Cash is what you must have to keep a business going and it isn't unusual for even a very successful business to run out of "cash" particularly as the business is growing.

cash discount
a deduction that is given for prompt payment of a bill. Even though the amount seems small, about 2 percent, when figured over a year it is important. A 2 percent discount for paying within 10 days is the same as getting 36 percent interest on your money for the year.

cash receipts
the money received by a business from customers. "Cash receipts" are to a business what food and water are to anything living. A business can survive just so long on its stored up capital.

contract
an agreement regarding mutual responsibilities between two or more parties. In business law a "contract" exists when there has been a meeting of minds - whether or not the contract is written. However, contracts are usually in written form but should never be taken lightly because they legally bind the parties to the agreement.

controllable expenses

those expenses that can be controlled or restrained - by the businessperson. Some of the costs of doing business can be postponed or spread out over a longer period of time. For example, depreciation on equipment is a "controllable" expense in the sense that it isn't required if one puts off obtaining new equipment until the level of business is such that it can support the new purchase and its depreciation allowance.

corporation

a business venture comprising an individual or a group of individuals treated by the law as an individual. A business corporation is an artificial personage, created by a charter, which can do business as a separate entity the same as individuals can do in a sole proprietorship or a partnership.

co-signers

joint signers of a loan agreement, pledging to meet the obligations in case of default. When you ask someone to "co-sign" a note, you are asking them to share a debt with you if you can't pay it back. They guarantee the loan will be paid back and the lender can take legal action to take their property if they refuse to pay.

credit

credits and debits are used in bookkeeping to record transactions. To credit is to place an entry on the right side of an account. A credit in an asset account makes it smaller. A credit in a liability account makes it larger. Another definition: The business owner's reputation for prompt payment of obligations, as in "a good credit rating."

D

debit

debits and credits are used in bookkeeping to record transactions. To debit is to place an entry on the left side of an account. A debit in a liability account makes it smaller. A debit in an asset account makes it larger.

debt

that which is owed. If you borrow money, buy something on credit or receive more money on an account than is owed, you have a "debt" - an obligation to pay back whatever amount of money or goods is involved. Going into "debt" was once considered a sin but can be a useful and often necessary way of doing business.

default

failure to pay a debt or meet an obligation. Any debt is a trust and failure to pay it is a violation of a high obligation.

demand

an order to comply with an obligation. In business we speak of paying on "demand". This simply means that the obligation must be satisfied immediately when requested. Contracts are often written with a "pay on demand" clause. This means just what it says: the debtor must pay when asked if the terms of the contract agreement have been met.

depreciation

a decrease in value through age, wear or deterioration. All of the equipment that you buy for a business begins to depreciate immediately and is worth something less as it continues to be used. Depreciation is a normal expense of doing business that must be taken into account.

E

entrepreneur

a person who organizes and manages a business.

equity capital

personal resources. In order to go into business, you must put up savings or property. You do it in hopes of getting a good return on your personal investment.

F

financing

obtaining money resources. Businesses usually have to obtain financing at some time - either to go into business or expand operations (hopefully not just to stay in business).

11

financial statements
documents that show your financial situation. Two major statements are needed to cover the information necessary to run a business and get financing. (Income statement and balance sheet.)

fixed expenses
those costs that don't vary from one period to the next. Generally, these are expenses that are not affected by the volume of business. Rent, for example, must be paid whether or not any business is accomplished.

franchise (franchisor, franchisee)
a right or privilege to deal in a certain line or brand of goods and services. A franchising company (franchisor) is in the business of "selling" businesses or brands to small businesspersons. Usually, the franchisor and the businessperson who agrees (franchisee) enter into a binding contract where the franchisor supplies the product, materials and a certain amount of know-how and the franchisee agrees to handle the product exclusively and run the business according to certain standards prescribed by the franchisor.

G

gross
overall total before deductions. Another way to put it is that "gross" means the whole amount. A businessperson has to learn early the difference between "gross" and "net" figures.

I

income
money coming in. In a business sense, "income" is really pretty much the same for the business as for an individual.

income statement
a financial document that shows how much money (revenues) came in and how much money (expenses) was paid out. Subtracting the expenses from the revenues gives you your profit and all three are shown on the income statement.

industry ratio
the standard or "average" percentage of expenses spent by firms in a similar type of business (i.e. firms in the same industry). These "industry ratio" figures are very important guidelines for a business.

interest
the cost of borrowing money. Just as you are interested in a return on your investment in your business, return on investment is a concern to the lender of money.

inventory
a list of assets being held for sale. If you are in a retail business, the stock you have on the shelves is "inventory" but then so are your available supplies, goods received or stored and any expendable items on hand.

invest
lay out money for any purpose from which a profit is expected. One way to evaluate whether an investment in a business is worthwhile is to consider what you would receive on that same amount of money put into a low risk investment.

itinerant seller
one who sells, services or negotiates a contract for the sale of goods or services at a place other than the seller's permanent place of business. Examples are home improvement, repairs of various types and door-to-door selling.

lease
a long term rental agreement. A "lease" arrangement is mutually advantageous to both the lessor (renter) and the lessee (one who rents). The agreement gives the landlord assurance that the property will be rented and protects the renter because it assures that the business property will not be rented out from under the business.

liability insurance
risk protection for actions for which a business is liable. Insurance that a business carries to cover the possibility of loss from lawsuits in the event the business or its agents were found at fault when an action occurred.

limited partnership

a legal partnership where some owners are allowed to assume responsibility only up to the amount invested. The idea for a limited partnership is that some investors may put up money for a business venture without being directly involved in its operation and so are not held responsible for the debts of the other partners beyond the possible loss of money they have invested.

liquidate

to settle a debt or to convert to cash. This literally means to do away with.

loan

money lent at interest. A lender makes a "loan" with the idea that it will be paid back as agreed and that interest will be paid as a sort of "rent" for the use of the money.

M

management

the art of conducting and supervising a business. It isn't enough to just invest money in a business - the business must be nurtured, protected and helped along to success. Managers do more than manage people, which most everyone understands, for they must also manage things.

marketing

all the activities involved in buying and selling a product or service. You must know most of the following things to market successfully:

- Who is going to buy?
- What is it they want?
- Where will they go to get it?
- How much will they pay?
- How much will they buy?
- How will you sell it?
- How much profit do you want?

merchandise

goods bought and sold in a business. "Merchandise" or stock is a part of inventory.

net
what is left after deducting all charges. (see "gross")

operating costs
expenditures arising out of current business activities. In other words, your "operating costs" for any period of time are what it cost you to do business - the salaries, electricity, rental, deliveries, etc., that were involved in performing the business dealings.

operating ratios
the relationship of costs from business activities. What percentage of your costs went for rent? How does it compare with other businesses like yours?

owner manager
one who owns and operates a business. One of the greatest assets that an "owner manager" has is flexibility to meet problems.

partnership
a legal business relationship of two or more people who share responsibilities, resources, profits, and liabilities. Partnerships are built on mutual trust and friendship, but should still have the agreement in writing.

payable
ready to be paid. One of the standard accounts kept by a bookkeeper is "accounts payable."

personnel
persons collectively in the employ of a business. As a small business grows, it will need people to handle the expansion of business and carry out the work of the business. Your personnel are a part of your business and deserve consideration as full-fledged members of the firm even though they may not share in the firm's ownership or profits.

plan
a plan is a formal decision to do something, then figuring out how you are going to do it before you start. You must answer the questions of what? where? when? how? and why? You should plan first then do. (See budget.)

posting
to enter in an account. Literally, "post" means to give a position to something, so when you "post" figures in a ledger, you are assigning them their right position in the firm's account books.

pricing
to set the selling price. One of the most difficult jobs in business is selecting the right price. Pricing should be done very carefully. You have to consider how much profit you need, what your competition is charging, and how much your customers are willing to pay.

principal
property or capital assets as opposed to income; also, one who is directly concerned in a business enterprise. This is another of those confusing words with more than one meaning, but if you really consider that it means "the first in importance," whether we are talking about people or capital assets, the meanings make more sense.

profit
financial gain; returns over expenditures. Simply put, "profit" is what you've got left after paying for everything.

profit margin
the difference between your selling price and your costs. A lot of factors affect profit margin both inside and outside the business. A reasonable profit margin is necessary to remain in business.

profit and loss statement
a list of the total amount of sales (revenues) and total costs (expenses). The difference between revenues and expenses is your profit or loss. It is also called an "income statement".

proprietorship
subject to exclusive ownership. A "proprietor" is one who owns a business and a business owned by one person is called a "proprietorship".

ratio
the relationship of one thing to another. A "ratio" is a shortcut way of comparing things that can be expressed as numbers or degrees.

receivable
ready for payment. When you sell on credit, you keep an "accounts receivable" as a record of what is owed to you and who owes it. In accounting, a "receivable" is an asset - it represents money that is owed to you.

reserve
that which is held back or stored for future use or in case of emergency. The success or failure of many young businesses depends on their abilities to weather a financial crisis.

retail
selling directly to the consumer. Selling in large quantities to dealers for resale is a "wholesale" activity, while selling in small quantities directly to people who will use the product is called "retail".

secured
protected or guaranteed. "Secure" means to make a thing safe, so when we speak of a "secured loan" we mean to make it safe or protect it by putting up something of value as collateral, as a guarantee of repayment.

service business
a retail business that deals in activities for the benefit of others.

terms of sale
the conditions concerning payment for a purchase. A very important source of saving.

tangible

something that is real. Literally, "tangible" means that the thing is such that you can touch it, but the meaning for business is something that can be seen and evaluated.

V

volume

an amount or quantity (of business). The "volume" of a business is the total it sells over a period of time.

W

wholesale

selling for resale. (See retail for explanation.)

SMALL BUSINESS ONTARIO

Start your small business library. For our helpful guidebooks to aid your business fill out this order card and mail today to:

Publications Ontario, Mail Orders,
5th Floor, 880 Bay St., Toronto, Ontario M7A 1N8
or telephone in Toronto—(416) 326-5300
toll free from other communities 1-800-668-9938

DETACH

Quantity

[ ]	Starting a Small Business in Ontario:	@ $3.00 $ _____
[ ]	How to Prepare a Business Plan for Manufacturing Businesses:	@ $6.00 $ _____
[ ]	How to Prepare a Business Plan for Service Businesses:	@ $6.00 $ _____
[ ]	How to Prepare a Business Plan for Retail Businesses:	@ $6.00 $ _____
[ ]	Record Keeping Made Easy:	@ $15.00 $ _____
[ ]	Marketing for a Small Manufacturing Business:	@ $6.00 $ _____
[ ]	Marketing for a Small Service Business:	@ $6.00 $ _____
[ ]	Marketing for a Small Retail Business:	@ $6.00 $ _____
[ ]	The State of Small Business 1990:	@ $5.00 $ _____

Sub-Total $ _____

Add GST (7%) $ _____

Total $ _____

_____
Name

_____
Business Name

_____
Address

_____
City   Province   Postal Code

[ ] CHEQUE OR MONEY ORDER ENCLOSED, PAYABLE TO *THE TREASURER OF ONTARIO*

CHARGE MY: [ ] VISA [ ] MASTER CARD

_____
Number   Expiry Date   Cardholder's Signature

Publications Ontario
Services des commandes postales
880, rue Bay, 5e étage
Toronto (Ontario)
M7A 1N8

Publications Ontario
Mail Orders
5th Floor
880 Bay Street
Toronto, Ontario
M7A 1N8

CHAPTER 2 :
THE BUSINESS

Once the decision has been made to enter into business,

and the type of business has been chosen, it is time to

decide how to begin.

This chapter discusses three different kinds of entrepreneurship: opening an entirely new business, buying an existing business, and operating a franchise. Each has its advantages, each its inherent disadvantages.

This chapter will also consider some of the basic factors of business and management common to all new companies.

THE NEW BUSINESS - STARTING FROM SCRATCH

This is the route chosen by most first-time entrepreneurs. Risk tends to be the highest in new business, but it offers the individual the greatest amount of personal freedom in determining company direction, new markets, or development of a new product or service.

Starting a business requires spending time on planning and clearly understanding how it will operate. Since most businesses start modestly, with low overhead and minimal staff, the owner manager very often must be all things to the business. This means long hours, having a clear understanding of all business aspects of the new enterprise and a need to follow a predetermined course. Failure to do so often leads to a breakdown in basic business functions, loss of control of the business's direction, and an inability to determine where the company stands in the marketplace. Those circumstances can lead to business failure at a very early stage.

It is important that the individual recognize personal limitations and thoroughly plan and understand the new business. This will greatly enhance the chances of success. In the end, a successful entrepreneur, having started from scratch and succeeded, will gain great satisfaction from the experience and achieve that level of freedom originally sought.

Some things to consider about starting from scratch:

Advantages
1. Potential lower overhead and lower start-up costs;
2. Greatest personal freedom;
3. Ability to enter new markets or introduce new products;
4. Ability to change business practices or direction quickly.

Disadvantages
1. Greatest risk;
2. Requires significant personal and business planning;
3. Clientele must be developed.

BUYING AN EXISTING BUSINESS

For the first-time business owner, an existing business offers many advantages such as an established clientele, a business method, perhaps inventory and premises and very often a reputable name. One very important question must be answered however; why is the business for sale?

Before purchasing a business, insist on reviewing financial statements for as many previous years as possible, up to five years, and obtain lists of clients/customers and suppliers. All leases and outstanding contracts must be reviewed. It is recommended that professional advice be sought to help complete the transaction (get an accountant to review financial information and a lawyer to review leases etc., in order to prepare the purchase agreement).

The two most important questions to ask are why is the business available and what is its true worth? The latter is a bit easier to answer, through professional advice/assessment. While this will be an added expense, an intelligent appraisal can go a long way to saving thousands of dollars.

Why the business is for sale and how good a risk it is are more difficult questions to answer. It is most important that as many questions as possible be answered before the transaction is complete.
- Why do I want to buy this business?
- Why does the owner want to sell?
- Does the business have a future?
- Will I feel comfortable and knowledgeable in operating this business?

20

Is all the information about the financial and customer aspects of the business readily available and willingly turned over by the seller?

Advantages	Disadvantages
1. Limited risk;	1. Product/service may be obsolete or market shrinking;
2. Significant personal freedom;	
3. Established service/product, clientele, method of operation, staff and name;	2. No growth potential;
	3. Accounts receivable may be too high or uncollectable;
4. Cash flow is being generated;	4. Seller may have hidden reasons for selling that have resulted in business deterioration over a period of years.
5. Relationship established with suppliers and banks.	

FRANCHISING

Entering the marketplace by "purchasing a franchise" can be one of the best ways for the entrepreneur to launch a successful business.

Franchising in Canada continues to grow at a significant rate. Franchise sales in Canada in 1987 were estimated at $61 billion; almost two-thirds of which are represented by the retail trade alone. It is expected that sales will increase 10 to 15 percent annually over the next few years.

There are good reasons for the rising popularity of the franchising method. In theory at least, the person who operates a franchise gets the best of two worlds - the freedom of running an independent business, coupled with the security of working for a large company. As well, he or she doesn't need to be a business expert to run a franchise successfully, because of the training systems and ongoing support that most franchisors continually provide. Best of all, the risk of failure can be a small fraction of that faced by an independent business. Please remember, however, that purchasing a franchise is not a guarantee of financial success for the franchisee.

What is Franchising?

Franchising is essentially a marketing technique used by many companies to distribute products and services. The franchisor supplies the product or service to the franchisee who in turn makes it available to the public.

Is Franchising for You?

Franchising isn't for everyone. To be successful in franchising requires you to fit within the framework of an established system. If you are too independent and too entrepreneurial to accept rules and regulations which someone else has instituted, then franchising may not be for you. It is a fundamental requirement of each franchise system that each unit within that system appears to be similar in every respect. Thus, you the franchisee must be a team player.

Investigate Before Investing:

Franchisors vary enormously as to their size and market experience. Some of the best known franchisors are large, well-established Canadian or international corporations, but many others are relatively small companies that have been started up quite recently. While size alone will not determine how well a franchisor supports its franchisees, joining a new franchise system, or one expanding into a new territory does represent a greater risk to a prospective franchisee. A new franchisor will not have the market presence of its established competitors. It may also still be in the process of developing its franchise system, and a full range of support services may not yet be in place. If the franchisor lacks the necessary resources, some of these services may never materialize. Therefore, in terms of the risk involved, there is a considerable difference between a mature franchisor with a successful track record in an established market and a new franchise system based on an unproven business concept.

Franchising is said to be like a marriage. It's intended to be a lasting relationship, therefore it is important you investigate and obtain answers to many questions before committing yourself to a franchise.

The best possible defence against the wrong investment is knowledge. Consequently you require detailed background information on the franchisor, its management, financial history, detailed information on the product or service and whether the franchise being offered is expanding or has limited growth potential.

While a franchisee might make a reasonable living, quite often he or she might not achieve the return envisaged. Before any commitments are made, the benefits and risks of being a franchisee should be fully analyzed in order to avoid a costly mistake.

It is imperative that you obtain the services of a good accountant and a franchise lawyer.

• Check the franchisor's credit background with Dun and Bradstreet and your banker. Also ensure that the Better Business Bureau has not received any major complaints against the franchisor.

• Request and analyze, if available, the franchisor's most recent financial statements. This is simple if the franchisor is a public company. Smaller franchisors, however, may not want to disclose such information so it may be necessary to rely on information from banks and other credit agencies.

• Obtain from the franchisor all the public information available on its operations. If it offers franchises in Alberta or in the United States, detailed documents have already been prepared and should be readily available. If, however, they are reluctant to give them to you, it is a bad sign. However, for smaller regional franchises in Canada, these documents may not exist.

• Ask for a copy of the franchisor's trademark application or registration. Without it, the franchisor can give you no assurance of its ability to protect its own trademark, which could lead to later problems.

• Request a list of all franchisees with their locations and telephone numbers. Discuss with a number of them the success and profitability of their outlets. Ask them how much time they spend on the business since this will affect their personal lifestyle. Also have these franchisees assess how well the franchisor has lived up to any promises. Do they feel they are getting something of value for their royalty payments?

• Complete the application or prescreening form if required by the franchisor. The franchisor should want to check out your financial background as carefully as you checked out their situation. If not, it is a bad sign.

• Obtain a full set of legal documents from the franchisor - the franchise agreement as well as registered user agreements, leases or subleases and assignment agreements.

- If a deposit is required, read the deposit agreement carefully and ensure that it is refundable. If not fully refundable, be sure that you will get at least 80-90% back. At this point, you must be satisfied with the franchisor's credibility and integrity.
- The franchisor should offer an acceptable site (if applicable) for your business. Visit the site and analyze any available descriptive material, paying special attention to surrounding population, average annual income and age distribution. For major investments exceeding $100,000, you may want to call in a professional to confirm the franchisor's report.
- Review the pro forma financial statements with an accountant.
- If your accountant has given you that green light, inform your banker fully about your plans. Obtain all the information about franchising available from the bank, as well as any specific financing packages related to the franchise you are buying. Discuss your eligibility for various loan programs available from the bank. Check to see whether the franchisor has an arrangement with a specific bank on financing.
- Inform your spouse and family completely about what you are doing. In most cases, your spouse will be required to guarantee the loan. In addition, you should assume that the whole family may also be physically and emotionally tied up in the business.
- Engage a lawyer who specializes in franchise-related matters to review all of the documents including trademark registration and the franchise agreement. As well, have an accountant take a final look at the franchise agreement as to any unfavourable tax implications.
- Finally, as the ultimate decision will rest with you, it is now time to apply as much common sense as possible. Try to answer objectively whether you are reasonably suited to the proposed franchise business. Are you willing to make a total commitment in order to succeed? Be honest with yourself - franchising isn't for everyone.

Seek Professional Help:
You will have done a lot of preliminary work yourself, however you will require the services of an accountant and a franchise lawyer. An accountant will review the costs and projections and determine if the bottom line makes sense. The accountant will wish to determine if the franchisor is financially stable. You do not want to buy into a financially troubled firm. Be extremely wary of franchisors when an analysis of their financial statements indicates their major source of revenue is franchise fees rather than franchise royalties. The conclusion would be that they are in business only to sell franchises as opposed to developing a viable franchise system.

The franchise lawyer will wish to review the franchise agreement which is the single most important document that you must deal with. It can be 10 pages, however others run to 40 to 50 pages.

There is help for you from different sources:

The Ontario Ministry of Consumer and Commercial Relations issues a booklet entitled "Facts about Franchising". It outlines the proper way to go about checking out a franchise/franchisor and the concept of franchising. It is available from:

Publications Ontario
880 Bay Street
Toronto, Ontario
M7A 1N8
Tel: (416) 326-5300
Toll-free 1-800-668-9938

The Canadian Franchise Association (most of the leading Canadian franchisors are members) can also offer valuable advice and assistance. It has published a booklet entitled "Investigate Before Investing". Contact:

Canadian Franchise Association
Suite 607, 88 University Avenue
Toronto, Ontario
M5J 1T6
Tel: (416) 595-5005

Small Business Ontario, Ministry of Industry, Trade & Technology provides an informative seminar "Purchasing a Franchise" in different communities throughout the province. This evening seminar will guide you through the steps and also answer your questions. Cost: $15.00. Contact the Small Business Hotline 1-800-567-2345 to obtain dates and locations.

LOCATION

Whether you are establishing a new business or purchasing an existing one, location is an important variable to consider. This may appear obvious, but it is very often neglected and is rarely part of the entrepreneur's business plan. Yet market strategy may evolve directly as a result of business location. Also, location cannot be decided by purely economic/business considerations. It is important to consider the residential, social and cultural opportunities of the community. This will have an impact on attracting future employees to your company or on reaching the target audience for your product or service.

There are many factors that will influence the location you choose. Proximity to market areas, sources of raw materials or supplies necessary, transportation systems and facilities and the availability of a skilled labour force are but a few to consider.

Ask yourself: Is it a growing community? What is the age make-up of the community?

The following is a short checklist of factors you should consider when deciding where to locate your business:

Zoning:
- Present zoning and future zoning?
- If it must be re-zoned what time span is involved and at what cost?

Building:
- Outside and inside appearance?
- Layout, lighting, heating, floors, acoustics, comfort, waste disposal, parking, landscape, snow removal?
- Outside storage - is it permitted?

Transportation:
- Shipping doors? Truck access?
- Any truck-road restrictions?
- Is there a truck terminal nearby?
- Is rail or air important?
- Is it on a bus route for your staff?

Utilities:
- Check your power supply, water, sewers, gas.
- What does each cost?
- Are they adequate?
- What would be required to upgrade them to your requirements?

Taxes:
- Present and future assessment for property taxes and business taxes.

Lease:
- Has it been checked by your lawyer?
- Is it too short or too long?
- Any options available?
- Who pays to have the lease drawn?
- What are you responsible for?
- What is the landlord responsible for?

Approvals:
- Will all government regulatory bodies approve your use of the building?
- Zoning, health, fire marshal, transportation, environment, labour.

Protection:
- Are there regular police patrols?
- What kind of fire protection?
- Hydrants nearby?
- Sprinkler system?
- Night guard?
- Any history of vandalism?

Neighbourhood:
- How stable is it? Getting better or getting worse?
- Are you compatible with the neighbours?
- Will you enjoy living nearby?

Restrictions:
- Are there protective covenants that will limit your sales?
- Any legal easements on your property?
- Can you grow physically in size?

Suppliers:
- Are you near them? Is it important?
- Can you get quick service when something breaks down?

Your customers:
- Who are they? Age, sex, income bracket.
- Where do they live, play, shop?
- What motivates them to buy your products?
- How often do they buy? Seasonal?
- Cash or credit?
- Can you afford to carry accounts receivable?

Your competition:
- How big, how old, how strong?
- What percentage of the market do they have?
- What advantages do you have?
- What advantages do they have?
- What percentage of the market will you get?

FINANCING AND VENTURE CAPITAL

As discussed in Chapter 1, financial planning is an important part of the overall planning process.

The success of your business will depend on you having sufficient capital to buy the equipment you need, acquire the inventory you will have to carry, pay overhead costs such as rents and salaries, and have a large enough reserve fund for extra working capital and to enable you to take advantage of "specials" or survive temporary setbacks.

It is essential to assess the cost of establishing and doing business, and determine the capital required before you begin.

Your funding requirements can be split into two main categories:

1. Initial costs - land, building, fixtures, machinery, supplies, vehicles, pre-opening expenses and opening inventory;
2. Daily operating costs - rising inventories, payroll, rents, taxes, advertising, accounts receivable.

It is vital that you know what all these costs will total. You must, therefore, prepare a cash flow forecast, which will give you a reasonably accurate estimate of your cash requirements for the first 12-month period. If you cannot do a cash flow forecast yourself, hire someone to do it for you.

The money you need to operate your business may come from several sources. These will include your own savings, perhaps loans from friends, relatives, investors, chartered banks or the Federal Business Development Bank. Other financial assistance may be available through lines of credit from your various suppliers.

SOURCES OF FINANCING

The most common source of financing for small business in Canada is the chartered banks. Under their operating terms of reference they can provide short term loans, long term mortgage loans or loans against inventory or accounts receivable, to provide working capital.

Chartered banks in Ontario provide a full range of banking services. These include personal and business deposit and loan accounts, buying and selling of foreign exchange, purchase and sale (or safekeeping) of securities and other valuables, letters of credit and the provision of market and credit information in Canada and other countries.

Other leading sources of finance are the insurance companies, trust companies, credit unions, commercial credit and acceptance companies, venture capital loan companies and factoring companies.

Leasing may also be considered. The interest rates are relatively high, but payments are totally deductible. Leasing is usually arranged for machinery, vehicles and office equipment, where it is best to avoid heavy capital cost outlays.

At the beginning, the most important financial sources will probably be yourself, friends, relatives, your own employees and suppliers, leasing and the banking system:

Notes:

- Internal sources include inventory control, cash management, credit management, etc.
- Friends are not usually the silent partners as originally perceived.
- Employees - are they the right ones to "lock in"?

BE SURE TO GET ENOUGH MONEY TO START

BOOKKEEPING

Failure to keep adequate records from the start is a problem that plagues many small businesses. Without records, there are no controls, and without controls, there can be no effective management. Lack of proper records can also be a source of major embarrassment in dealing with banks, and can lead to difficulties with tax departments and other areas where government agencies are involved.

The MITT publication, "Record Keeping Made Easy" is a simplified step-by-step guide to establishing an effective small business record system. Copies are available for $15.00 each through Publications Ontario or your nearest Ministry of Industry, Trade and Technology Business Self-Help office. (See mail order card in this book.)

CREDIT CONTROL

Maintaining a proper cash flow is probably the single most important factor in operating a successful business.

According to the president of one of Canada's leading collecting agencies, cash flow problems can be avoided by making sure that you are paid promptly for services rendered or goods sold. Statistics show that the longer an account goes unpaid, the greater the risk that it will not be paid in full. Therefore, the control and collection of accounts receivable is most important.

Unless you are paid in advance, you always run a risk of not being paid. This risk can be minimized by taking proper precautions.

Here are a few important items:
- Know your customer;
- Make sure the terms are clearly understood;
- Bill promptly;
- Demonstrate that you expect prompt payment;
- Maintain dated accounts receivable;
- Follow up on the payment if not received as planned.

GOVERNMENT SUPPORT

In support of economic development the federal and Ontario government have established lending agencies to work with small business.

The Federal Business Development Bank (FBDB) is a Crown corporation established by an act of Parliament to promote and assist in the development of business enterprises in Canada by providing them with financial and management services.

The purpose of the bank is to supplement rather than compete with other financial institutions. For this reason it is generally considered a secondary source of financing.

The FBDB functions purely as a business bank and does not provide deposit or chequing facilities to the general public.

Its purpose is to provide financial assistance to sound commercial or industrial enterprises that are unable to obtain required capital from the regular sources on conditions or terms reasonable to their operation.

The FBDB also provides an excellent management counselling service, conducts management training seminars in cities and towns across Canada and publishes booklets on a wide range of topics pertaining to the management of small business.

Listings of local FBDB offices can be found in the white pages of the telephone directory.

31

Ontario's three development corporations, Ontario Development Corporation (ODC), Northern Ontario Development Corporation (NODC) and Eastern Ontario Development Corporation (EODC), offer a comprehensive program of financial and advisory services to business and industry throughout Ontario.

Secondary manufacturing industries, service industries closely allied to manufacturing, tourist operations and tourist attractions are all eligible for development corporation assistance.

The financial assistance provided will be tailored to the needs of the applicant through any one or a combination of the following methods:

• Corporation consultants may help the client in approaching private lenders or other sources of government funding.

• Guarantees can be provided to encourage private lender participation.

• Direct loans from the development corporations involving a variety of terms and conditions of repayment can be adapted to meet the specific needs of the small business owner.

• Special incentives may be offered to ensure that a proposal with the potential for significant economic benefit to the province has an opportunity to succeed, and that there is a demonstrated need by the client and the province for such an incentive.

• Ontario Development Corporation:

Hamilton
Bank of Montreal Tower
1 James Street North
Suite 200
Hamilton, Ontario
L8R 2K3
Tel: (416) 521-7785

Kitchener
30 Duke Street West
Suite 906
Kitchener, Ontario
N2H 3W5
Tel: (519) 744-1991

London
195 Dufferin Avenue
Suite 607
London, Ontario
N6A 1K7
Tel: (519) 433-2871

Metro Toronto
5 Fairview Mall Drive
Suite 480
Willowdale, Ontario
M2J 2Z1
Tel: (416) 491-7996

Orillia
73 Mississaga Street East
P.O. Box 746
Orillia, Ontario
L3V 6K7
Tel: (705) 325-5553

Peel
4 Robert Speck Parkway
Suite 1140
Mississauga, Ontario
L4Z 1S1
Tel: (416) 279-9150

Toronto
56 Wellesley Street West
5th Floor
Toronto, Ontario
M7A 2E7
Tel: (416) 326-1070

• Eastern Ontario Development Corporation:

Kingston
Ontario Government
Building
1055 Princess Street
Suite 308
Kingston, Ontario
K7L 5T3
Tel: (613) 545-4445

Ottawa
Place de Ville
Tower B
850-112 Kent Street
Ottawa, Ontario
K1P 5P2
Tel: (613) 566-3707

Pembroke
Registry Office Building
400A Pembroke Street East
Pembroke, Ontario
K8A 3K8
Tel: (613) 735-2306

Peterborough
139 George Street North
Peterborough, Ontario
K9J 3G6
Tel: (705) 742-3490

• Northern Ontario Development Corporation:

Kenora
227 Second Street South
Kenora, Ontario
P9N 1G1
Tel: (807) 468-2843

North Bay
147 McIntyre Street West
North Bay, Ontario
P1B 2Y5
Tel: (705) 472-4900

Sault Ste. Marie
500 Bay Street
Sault Ste. Marie, Ontario
P6A 1X4
Tel: (705) 945-8300

Timmins
273 Third Avenue
Timmins, Ontario
P4N 1E2
Tel: (705) 264-1323

Sudbury
Ontario Government
Building
199 Larch Street
Sudbury, Ontario
P3E 5P9
Tel: (705) 675-4333

Thunder Bay
435 James Street South
Thunder Bay, Ontario
P7C 5G6
Tel: (807) 475-5322

VENTURE CAPITAL

Venture capital is long-term and risk capital. Companies providing venture capital take an equity position, usually a minority one in the 20 to 40 percent range. In addition, they can usually provide advice and consultation on such matters as financial planning and control, underwriting, accounting and marketing. Because it takes a minority position, the venture capital company normally prefers firms that have management with proven ability and where the lack of long-term financing appears to be the major factor inhibiting the establishment or growth of the client's enterprise.

While the owners remain in control, most venture capital companies require a seat on the board of directors of the company and a measure of control over such matters as key employee salaries and insurance, payment of dividends or the making of the major capital expenditures without prior agreement.

The Ontario government's Small Business Development Corporations program is designed to stimulate private sector investment in small businesses. This program provides attractive financial incentives to individuals and corporations that invest funds in Small Business Development Corporations. These corporations, in turn, invest money in certain eligible small businesses. The corporations, while subject to Ontario corporations income tax, are exempt from the capital tax.

For details, contact the Ministry of
Revenue.

Telephone enquiries:
> (Call toll free) in Oshawa - (416) 433-6469
> In Metro Toronto - (416) 965-1160, ext. 6469
> All other areas - dial 1-800-263-7965.

Written enquiries:
> Ministry of Revenue
> Ontario Small Business Development
> Corporations
> 33 King Street West
> Oshawa, Ontario
> L1H 8H9

Information is also available through the
Ministry of Industry, Trade and Technology's field offices
and Business Self-Help offices.

LEASING

Whether your new business venture requires retail space,
industrial space, office space or a combination of any or all
of the three, the choice of premises is one of your first
major business decisions.

You must choose the right location, the
right size to meet your requirements at the right price or
lease rate. Remember that you will be locked into an
agreement for one to five years or longer, so make your
decision carefully.

Obtain the best information and advice possible. Unless you are an expert in these matters yourself,
this would be the right time to consult a qualified, reputable real estate firm that specializes in commercial/indus-
trial leasing.

Leasing Retail Space

Having selected a potential location, your
next consideration is size.

If you require a small space, keep in mind
that it is very difficult to find good street-front space
under 800 square feet. Therefore, if you are thinking
small, you will almost certainly be in an indoor mall.

You will find that the smaller retail spaces command much higher rates per square foot, as they are generally located in high traffic areas. The compensating factor is that, because of this heavier traffic and greater exposure to impulse buyers, you may be able to achieve greater sales dollars per square foot.

Most people think they need more space than they actually do. Good space planning and merchandising techniques can bring your requirements into proper perspective.

Types of Leases

The terminology involved in commercial and industrial leasing can be confusing to the inexperienced. The most common form of retail lease, however, is generally quoted at so much per square foot or metre, per annum - "wholly net against percentage" - with the total being divided into 12 equal payments.

Wholly net means that all operating costs (such as heating, electricity, taxes, etc.) are paid by the tenant, whether they are metered directly or charged on a proportionate share basis.

Against percentage refers to the fact that the rate is being quoted as the greater of either x dollars per square foot or square metre per annum or a stated percentage of gross annual sales, wholly net (usually 6 percent to 8 percent for most retailers).

Rates are the result of many factors, and will vary from town to town, from region to region and even from one section of a city or town to another. Here the services of a good realtor will be extremely helpful. The realtor will be thoroughly familiar with all of the local rates and will be able to help you arrive at a sound decision.

Industrial Space

The leasing of space for light industrial use is no different than that of most other business transactions: first you must know your requirements, and then you must be aware of the terms of the agreement binding the transaction.

36

Carefully consider your particular type of business. Ask yourself: of the total space, how much should be devoted to warehouse or manufacturing and how much to office use? A good rule of thumb is that the ratio of office to warehouse/manufacturing is roughly 1 to 10.

Once you have pinpointed the total space requirement, clearly define physical space layout. Ceiling height is critical. Perhaps for your business cubic measurement (for stacking of inventory) is much more important than square footage.

Yet another consideration is the method of shipping the product. If truck level shipping is required, the floor of the plant must be level with the floor of the truck. However, if grade level shipping is your choice, the plant floor must be level with the outside driveway.

In the search for suitable space, you will probably come across the industrial condominium, a concept similar to that found in the residential sector. While there are many advantages here, such as equity build-up and the availability of significant tax advantages, there are limitations. Industrial condominium space is normally not less than 500 square metres. Therefore, to consider a condominium, you must be fairly certain that your space requirement will remain constant. If at a later date you find you must expand, you will have to sell, perhaps at a time that will interfere with the smooth operation of your business.

OWNING YOUR PREMISES

Faced with the increasing cost of leasing space, many small- and medium-sized businesses have considered ownership.

Today ownership has become a possibility for the small business owner. You must ask yourself whether the concept is valid for your particular business.

In order to fully appreciate the financial advantages of ownership, consider the following:

In the past, it was possible to obtain fixed leases for up to 20 years. With such leases, the financial benefits of owning versus leasing were minimal. However, given current economic conditions, there are several built-

37

in benefits to owning over leasing.

• Tax benefits -

These include deductions of interest payments on any financing plus capital cost allowance or
depreciation of owning.

• Capital appreciation -

Given the state of the economy today, it is
reasonable to expect a substantial increase in the value of
commercial real estate in the future.

• Equity build-up -

If the ownership is financed by any form
of debt financing, such as mortgage (which is usually the
case), repayment of the principal constitutes equity build-
up to the point when the real estate is owned 100 percent
over time.

• Cash flow -

In an equity position, it is often possible to
generate cash flow by leasing space to tenants.

There are other benefits for the owner of
office space, including control over long term planning of
office accommodation and the opportunity to use office
space as an asset for personal corporate retirement funding.

When deciding whether to lease or buy
there is one final consideration. Items such as company
cars, trucks, fixtures and equipment can either be bought
or leased. This is a good way to ease cash flow problems.
There are two major advantages: first, significant capital
outlay can be avoided and second, the entire cost of leasing
can be used as a cost of doing business when reporting
income for taxation purposes.

Over the years, economists and accountants have developed hundreds of business ratios to assist them in evaluating the financial health of businesses. Several have been proven. Here are some that may help you put things in proper perspective.

Total Current Assets
Total Current Liabilities

Current Ratio: This relationship gauges how well the business is able to pay current debts using only its current assets. It is also called the Working Capital Ratio. By rule of thumb it should be 2 to 1 (or 200 percent or $2 to $1). The higher it is, the better the indication, but the actual quality and management of assets must be considered.

Cash + Accounts Receivable
(+ any other quick assets)
Current Liabilities

Quick Ratio: Popularly called the Acid Test Ratio, rule of thumb says this one should be 1 to 1 (or 100 percent or $1 to $1). This ratio indicates the extent to which a company could pay current debt without relying on future sales. Quick assets are highly liquid - those which are immediately convertible to cash. In addition to accounts receivable, they include marketable securities.

Any Operating Expense x 100
Net Sales

Operating Expense Ratios: Business owners gain valuable management information by separately dividing each operating expense, such as salaries or wages, by net sales. From the resulting picture, owners can evaluate internal economic efficiency.

Total Debt (or Liabilities)
Total Equity (or Net Worth)

Debt to Equity: This ratio compares the amount invested in the business by creditors with that invested by the owner(s). The higher the ratio, the more the creditors' claim - possibly indicating that the business is extending its debt beyond its ability to repay. For example, at 1 to 5, debt is only 20 percent of equity; at 1 to 1, debt is 100 percent; at 5 to 1, it is 500 percent. However, an extremely low ratio may indicate that the owner is too conservative and is not letting the business realize its potential.

Net Income (or Profit)
Total Equity (or Net Worth)

Net Income to Equity: A measurement of the owner's, partner's, or shareholder's rate of return on investment, this ratio is almost always given as a percentage. It shows the interest rate that the income yields on the investment, and is an important yardstick of profitability and management efficiency.

Net Sales
Inventory

Sales to Inventory: This is a measurement of the relationship between inventory and sales to help determine inventory turnover. This ratio is important in determining the investment to be made in inventory and maintaining a watch on dated stock. The aim here is to maintain and increase sales while inventory is reduced or at least maintained.

Net Profits
Sales

Net Profit to Sales: This is a profit margin measurement to help determine management's ability to control expenses, pay taxes and result in a reasonable profit margin on sales. A high profit margin is the desirable test here. Operating expenses kept under control through efficient management will result in a constant ratio over several years.

Sales
Net Worth

Sales to Net Worth: This is a measurement of volume of sales in relation to the business's investment. It is important to keep a balance; high sales to worth puts pressure on the investment and loss of sales means underutilizing capital, making return on investment low.

Ratio of Receivables x 365
Sales

Average Collection period: A quick analysis of receivables, this management tool determines the efficiency of this firm's collection capabilities, its relative receivable position and bad debt or receivable write-offs.

These ratios are of value only when compared to industry averages in similar sectors. To obtain comparative data, contact your accountant, who will be able to obtain such information, or refer to firms such as Dun & Bradstreet who produce industry averages and ratios on an annual basis.

The following is a guide to determining the need for a particular type of retail business in a community. The information has been obtained from the United States Department of Commerce, Census Bureau, and represents American averages. A caution in using these statistics: they are meant as a guide only. These are U.S. figures, which very often reflect larger metropolitan areas and may not be consistent with trade areas and practices in Ontario. They should not be used as the sole basis for determining the type of business to establish or the kind of community in which the business should be established.

Number of Inhabitants to Support Store
(by selected kinds of business)

Kinds of business	Number of inhabitants, per store
Food Stores	
Grocery stores	1,348
Meat & fish (seafood) market	14,589
Fruit stores, vegetable market	34,869
Candy, nut, confectionery stores	25,466
Dairy product stores	32,116
Bakery products stores	10,212
Eating, Drinking Places	
Eating places	751
Drinking places (alcoholic beverages)	2,833
General Merchandise	
Department stores	22,698
General merchandise stores	10,645
Variety stores	16,809
Apparel, Accessory Store	
Family clothing stores	9,574
Shoe stores	5,756
Women's clothing specialty stores and furriers	3,856
Children's, infants'-wear store	34,278
Men's and boys' wear	12,198
Furriers and fur shops	119,486

42

Furniture: Home Furnishings, Appliance Dealers

Furniture; home furnishing stores	5,915
Household appliances, radio TV stores	16,287
Music stores, records and musical instruments	18,542

Automotive Groups

Passenger car dealers (new & used)	8,336
Passenger car dealers (used only)	6,556
Gasoline service stations	1,672
Tire, battery, accessory dealers	4,638
Boat dealers	41,371
Household trailer dealers	40,735
Motorcycle dealers	33,374

Lumber, Building Materials

Lumber, building materials dealers	7,936
Paint, glass, wallpaper stores	19,547
Hardware stores	8,930
Nurseries, lawn and garden supply	13,732

Other Retail Stores

Drug and proprietary stores	4,355
Jewelry stores	5,859
Book stores	15,236
Stationery stores	34,540
Sporting goods and bicycle stores	6,535
Florists	6,528
Cigar stores, stands	65,325
News dealers, news stands	17,280
Camera, photographic supply stores	33,975
Luggage, leather goods stores	70,008
Hobby, toy stores	10,285
Gift, novelty, souvenir stores	5,468

Source: Bureau of the Census, US Department of Commerce 1982 Census of Retail Trade

One of the most important resources available to small business is the local professional advisor - the banker, accountant, bookkeeper, lawyer and management consultant. Small business owners, especially at the early development stages, tend to under-utilize these professionals.

All charge for advice or service given except the banker, who earns income through the financial services provided. Many new entrepreneurs are concerned about the cost of the service rather than the potential benefits. Yet the cost of professional help is a legitimate business expense (tax deductible) and a beneficial investment in successful management techniques and a well run business.

The Banker

The single most important person to a small business is the banker. Bankers provide necessary capital and sound business advice. Banking in Canada is a competitive business; services and levels of expertise vary from bank to bank and branch to branch, so don't be afraid to shop around.

Be prepared to be open and friendly with your banker. The more information you provide and the better you keep your banker informed the easier it will be to deal with the bank and receive the desired service.

Develop good bank relationships by doing the following:

- give the bank manager all the information required for approval of the loan;
- arrange a line of credit to meet peak requirements - but borrow only what is necessary, when it is necessary;
- adjust the loan level as actual requirements change;
- make realistic repayment commitments;
- avoid overdrafts and excesses;
- be prepared to provide security for the loan.

information:
The lender will require the following

- amount of loan and the term or period for which it is required;
- reason for desiring loan;
- brief history of company;
- financial statements of business for past three years;
- details of current financial position, including specific data on:
    - accounts receivable
    - accounts payable
    - inventory
    - fixed assets
    - short and long term debt
    - special accounts
- facts about company operations;
- facts about management and officers of company;
- details of project to be financed (if applicable);
- financial data on operating results of new project (if applicable);
- effect of loan - projected cash flow and projected financial statements;
- security offered.

collateral:
The lender may accept the following as

- personal guarantees of officers of limited companies;
- general assignment of accounts receivable;
- pledging of cash surrender value of life insurance;
- agreement to restrict salaries, drawings and loan payments of proprietors, partners and principal shareholders;
- granting of a floating charge debenture;
- mortgages and general security agreements.

The Lawyer

Establishing a small business, making changes to an existing one, or buying or selling a business require careful study, and it is often advisable to obtain legal help.

Your lawyer can provide research and advice, and properly close a partnership agreement, an incorporation, a sale or purchase of business, etc.

The lawyer is working for you, so be sure to take time in deciding who to hire. You should feel comfortable when dealing with your lawyer. Your needs must be clearly understood. Therefore, it is most important that the lawyer be a business lawyer and deliver easily what you ask. At no time should you assume everything is under control and all work completed. It is your responsibility to check all documents, read all clauses and understand fully what you are signing or accepting. Do not put yourself in the position of trying to save a few dollars by performing your own legal functions, especially if you are unsure or have never dealt with these issues before. Legal fees are normal business expenses and may result in valuable savings in the long run.

The Accountant

A good accountant can be looked upon as another valuable member of your management team. Many small business owners view their accountant simply as the person who puts their income tax information together once a year. The accountant can provide you with much more.

Shop around for an accounting firm or accountant much the same way you look for a lawyer. Find a firm that is interested in your business and not just your account. Most small businesses are not receiving adequate service, mostly because they don't ask. An accounting firm that provides ongoing financial information (at least on a monthly basis) and helps you interpret the information and advises accordingly is very important to you. This cannot be stressed strongly enough: you, the owner, must be able to review the financial status of your business at any time so that you can make the necessary business decisions.

The exchange of information in the business world is vital. Equally important is ensuring the confidentiality of such information by making it available only to bona fide commercial operators who will use it as a working tool and respect the need to maintain discretion.

Business Reports

A number of companies provide a reporting service. Their client's confidence is protected in much the same way. The information is available only to subscribers to their service, and the subscribers must be accredited business organizations.

One of the better known and most widely used services of this type is the Dun & Bradstreet report.

Newcomers to the business world seeking information on a specific business operation (such as buying an existing business) may request that their bank manager obtain this information for them. Banks will usually comply if they are satisfied that the information is to be used solely for the purpose of evaluation and will be kept confidential.

Credit Bureaus

Credit bureaus, operating in Canada since 1922, now have more than 150 branches and a staff of more than 2,000 to provide businesses with consumer credit records of individuals.

Credit bureaus confirm information that credit grantors (banks, mortgage companies, department stores, oil companies, finance companies and automobile dealers) have obtained from individuals requesting consumer credit under Canada's consumer credit laws. Any individual applying for credit must do so in writing. When consumers do this, they supply information such as details of identification, present and past addresses, present and past employment, salaries and references to the grantor. At the same time, they agree to their applications being checked. The credit bureaus collect information from reports of other credit requests by the consumer, turndowns of credit and payment histories obtained from existing accounts where credit was granted.

Other information on the credit bureau's files - not supplied from the credit grantors - is derived from the public record: judgements, non-responsibility

47

notices, registered chattel mortgages, conditional sales and bankruptcies.

To use the credit bureaus' services, a business must apply to the nearest office and, depending on whether the market is local or national, take out a membership. With the annual membership comes a special code number that allows the business to telephone the credit bureau and obtain verbal reports on individuals. A nominal fee is charged for each report. Written reports can also be obtained.

THE COMPUTER FROM DAY ONE

At first thought, a computer may seem like an unaffordable and needless expense for your start up business. But there are, in fact, several reasons to have a·computer from the start.

Even before your business has opened its doors, you can use a computer to prepare your business plan and presentation to your investors and lenders.

You can use a computer and spreadsheet software to explore a range of what ifs that will show the effect of various changes in income and costs. What if interest rates on business loans change? What if cash flow is delayed by slow payments? What if operating costs go up or down by various percentages? What if you rent or lease for different durations at different rates? What if your projected sales reach different levels and how will this relate to all the other what ifs?

This detailed approach to your new business, presented in a quality, printed form, will impress potential lenders and investors with your professionalism and thoroughness.

At this early stage of putting together your business you may not have the cash to own your own computer. You might then consider renting or leasing the system you need.

About $100 a month

There have been tremendous improvements in the price/performance ratio of small computers. You can lease an entry-level, state-of-the-art desktop computer, with three frequently used software solutions for a small business; spreadsheet, basic accounting and word processing, for about $100 a month.*

By factoring a computer into your new business costs, you can build in a powerful tool for the management and marketing aspects of your business.

Accurate and timely management

Earlier this booklet said, "Failure to keep adequate records from the start is a problem that plagues many small businesses". Your own computer, by taking the repetitive work out of your record keeping, can not only speed up the work, it can provide an incentive to get it done on time because it makes data entry so much easier.

Timely record keeping will help you stay on top of changes that can affect your profitability. It can improve your control of costs, and control is the basis of effective management.

A computer can flag over- or under-stocking of inventory, reveal what is moving and what isn't, show you trends as they develop and help you stay ahead of slow-paying accounts.

Your banker and the various tax departments of government may be easier to deal with if your records are complete and comprehensible.

What is more, by doing accurate record keeping yourself, you could pay your accountant for time spent providing advice to you versus time spent on record . keeping.

Time saving and productivity

Many businesses require the preparation of lengthy documents with large quantities of text and figures. Getting them right can take forever without a computer, especially when changes require you to start all over again.

A desktop computer with a good word processing program will allow you to set up the basic document, then revise the numbers, or specific words and sentences or even move paragraphs around without starting from the beginning each time things change. For frequently used documents such as price lists or contracts you can update or customize with a minimum investment of time.

*Based on a 60 month extended term lease.

Especially at the beginning of your business when you and your colleagues are doing all the chief cook and bottle washer jobs, time you don't use for preparing documents is time you can use for building the business.

There are many ways a small computer can improve your productivity.

In one music store, the owner built a database listing all customers and their choice of music and media (e.g. record, tape, compact disk). As new shipments arrive, employees use quiet time to compare the new music with the database and call customers about appropriate new arrivals. Sales increase and customers are impressed by the service - an important factor when you remember that competitive music stores carry the same music.

There are many examples of how a computer can be used to help you promote business, instead of waiting for it. And there are many professionals including authorized computer dealers and software developers who can provide advice on how to use a computer to its advantage in your business.

Why now? Why not later?

You may say, "My business will be too small for a computer when I start up. I'll get one later". People may once have said that about a typewriter.

The fact is that it can be more efficient to begin with a computer. You need not develop manual systems that have to be converted - inevitably - to a computer. And you can have a powerful marketing resource at your command.

A computer can be an inexpensive and valuable tool.

A free booklet produced by IBM Canada Ltd. offers valuable information on investing in a computer for your business. You can call IBM at 1-800-465-1234 to receive your own copy of "How to Buy a Computer for a Small Business".

IBM is a registered trade-mark of International Business Machines Corporation. IBM Canada Ltd., a related company, is a registered user.

PLEASE HELP US TO SERVE YOU BETTER

Please give us a moment of your time. You can help us improve our services.
Simply tear out this reply card, fill in the information, fold, seal and mail.
Thank you.

DETACH

Ministry of Industry, Trade & Technology
Ontario

Small Business Ontario

| 0 | 1 |

PLEASE PRINT

SURNAME

GIVEN NAME

NAME OF YOUR BUSINESS (if already registered)

ADDRESS (Business or home) - (Indicate number, street, apt./suite)

CITY

POSTAL CODE

TELEPHONE

Area Code

NOTE: ENTER APPROPRIATE LETTER IN BOX AT RIGHT, WHERE APPLICABLE

SEX

M or F

AGE GROUP

A. UNDER 30   B. 30-50   C. OVER 50

BUSINESS STATUS

CURRENTLY
A. OPERATING

INVESTIGATING
B. POSSIBLE START-UP

PLANNING START-UP WITHIN
C. MAXIMUM 3 MONTHS

BUSINESS TYPE

A. SERVICE   B. RETAIL   C. MANUFACTURING

EMPLOYEES

HOW MANY EMPLOYEES, OTHER THAN YOURSELF, WILL YOU BE STARTING WITH?
OR, IF YOU ARE CURRENTLY IN OPERATION,
HOW MANY EMPLOYEES DO YOU PRESENTLY HAVE?

FULL TIME   PART TIME

INVESTMENT

HOW MUCH MONEY WILL YOU BE INVESTING/HAVE YOU INVESTED, IN YOUR BUSINESS?

| $4,999 | $5,000 - | $10,000 - | $15,000- | $20,000 |
| A. OR LESS | B. $9,999 | C. $14,999 | D. $19,999 | E. AND OVER |

SALES

IF YOU ARE CURRENTLY OPERATING A BUSINESS,
WHAT ARE YOUR TOTAL ESTIMATED SALES FOR THE NEXT 12 MONTH PERIOD?

| $24,999 | $25,000 - | $100,000 - | $250,000- | $500,00 | N/A - BUSINESS IN OPERATION |
| A. OR LESS | B. $99,999 | C. $249,999 | D. $499,999 | E. AND OVER | F. LESS THAN A YEAR |

BUSINESS REGISTRATION

HOW WILL/HAS YOUR BUSINESS BE/BEEN REGISTERED?

SOLE
A. PROPRIETORSHIP

B. PARTNERSHIP

C. CORPORATION

Personal information contained on this form is collected under the authority of the Ministry of Industry and Trade Act, S.O. 1982, c.31, s.3 and s.6 and will be used to provide statistical information on entrepreneurs in order to study small business trends in Ontario. Questions about this collection should be directed to: Small Business Ontario, 7th Floor, Hearst Block, 900 Bay Street, Toronto, M7A 2E1, Telephone: (416) 965-5494.
1194 (08/89)

DETACH

29807

Postage will be paid by

Ministry of Industry, Trade and Technology
Small Business Ontario
7th Floor, Hearst Block
900 Bay Street
Toronto, Ontario
M7A 9Z9

CHAPTER 3: REGULATIONS, REGISTRATIONS, INCORPORATIONS AND LICENCES

All businesses, large and small, are subject to certain laws and regulations. These are designed for the good of the public and the protection of the consumer. Some are laid down by the municipality, some by the provincial government, some by the federal government, and others by regulatory bodies set up to ensure that products offered for sale conform to required safety and other standards.

SMALL BUSINESS AND THE LAW

Other regulations are designed for the benefit and protection of the rights of employees - and then, of course, there are the various tax regulations. Most of these regulations are dealt with briefly in this publication. For more detailed information the reader should consult the office responsible for the administration of the specific regulation.

REGISTRATION OF A NAME

Sole Proprietorship Registration

A sole proprietorship is not required to be registered if the business is carried on under the owner's name. If the business uses a name other than the owner's or adds "and Company" or other words, a declaration must be filed under the Partnership Registration Act within 60 days with:

Information Services
Companies Branch
Ministry of Consumer and
Commercial Relations
393 University Avenue
2nd Floor
Toronto, Ontario
M7A 2H6
Tel: (416) 593-8880

The registration of the name does not in itself ensure exclusive use of that name in Ontario for the individual registering it. The ministry has no obligation to avoid name duplication or to advise anyone registering a name that it has been previously registered.

You are responsible for ensuring that the name is not already in use. Upon request and for a fee, the Ministry of Consumer and Commercial Relations will check its files and provide the addresses for any duplicates that may exist.

ARTICLES OF INCORPORATION

Persons wishing to incorporate a business must file with:
Corporate Services Section
Companies Branch
Ministry of Consumer and
Commercial Relations
393 University Avenue
2nd Floor
Toronto, Ontario
M7A 2H6
Tel: (416) 596-3757

Articles of Incorporation may also be delivered to the Land Registry offices in the following municipalities:

Barrie	Oshawa	Sudbury
Hamilton	Ottawa	Thunder Bay
Kingston	Peterborough	Welland
Kitchener	Sarnia	Windsor
London	Sault Ste. Marie	

Addresses can be found in the blue pages of your telephone directory.

Articles must be accompanied by a NUANS name search report. It is the responsibility of the group seeking incorporation to conduct its own name search. The Ontario Ministry of Consumer and Commercial Relations does not undertake these searches.

A number of private companies provide this service. Most are capable of doing a Canada-wide computer name search within a 24 hour period. These companies are listed in the Yellow Pages under "Searchers of Records".

Corporations are required to file an Initial Notice or Notice of Change Form 1, Corporations Information Act, with the Ministry of Consumer and Commercial Relations, Corporate Services Section, within 60 days of incorporation.

Co-operatives

Persons wishing to register a co-operative venture should contact:

Ministry of Financial Institutions
Credit Unions and Cooperatives
Services Branch
555 Yonge Street
6th Floor
Toronto, Ontario
M7A 2H6
Tel: (416) 326-9300

Proposed names for co-operatives must be approved by the ministry. An approved name will be cleared for a period of 90 days for a fee of $15.

When the co-operative is a non-profit no-gains co-operative, special clauses are contained in the articles. The registration fee for this type of co-operative is $100.

For a co-operative covered by other articles, the registration fee is $500. Applicants should seek legal assistance in the preparation of the required articles.

Non-profit, non-share co-operatives are incorporated under the Co-operative Corporations Act. The group seeking incorporation must conduct its own name search. The Ontario Ministry of Consumer and Commercial Relations does not undertake these searches.

PARTNERSHIPS AND
LIMITED PARTNERSHIP
REGISTRATION

Partnerships must be registered under the Partnerships Registration Act by filing a declaration within 60 days at the Companies Branch at the address previously given.

In a limited partnership, partners are liable only to the extent of the capital they have contributed. A limited partner becomes a general partner if he or she takes part in the management of the partnership. For details, refer to the Limited Partnership Act, available at:

Publications Ontario
880 Bay Street
Toronto, Ontario
M7A 1N8

WHERE TO
INCORPORATE

When a corporation intends to operate or have branch operations in more than one province, a federal incorporation may be advantageous.

However, if a corporation intends to operate primarily in one province, it may be preferable to incorporate in that province. Extra-provincial corporations must be licensed or registered in any other provinces in which they wish to do business.

Corporations that incorporated federally and are doing business in Ontario are required to file an Initial Notice or Notice of Change Form within 60 days upon entering the province.

WHAT FORM OF
BUSINESS
ORGANIZATION?

Sole Proprietiorship

Advantages
1. Low start-up costs.
2. Greatest freedom from regulation.
3. Owner in direct control.
4. Minimal working capital requirements.
5. Tax advantage to small owner.
6. All profits to owner.

Disadvantages
1. Unlimited liability.
2. Lack of continuity.
3. Difficult to raise capital.

Partnership

Advantages
1. Ease of formation.
2. Low start-up costs.
3. Additional sources of venture capital.
4. Broader management base.
5. Possible tax advantage.
6. Limited outside regulation.

Disadvantages
1. Unlimited liability.
2. Lack of continuity.
3. Divided authority.
4. Difficulty in raising additional capital.
5. Hard to find suitable partners.

Corporation

Advantages
1. Limited liability.
2. Specialized management.
3. Ownership is transfer-able.
4. Continuous existence.
5. Legal entity.
6. Possible tax advantages.
7. Easier to raise capital.

Disadvantages
1. Closely regulated.
2 Most expensive form to organize.
3. Charter restrictions.
4. Extensive record keeping necessary.
5. Double taxation.

FEDERAL INCORPORATION

Federal incorporation is effected under the Canada Business Corporations Act by filing articles of incorporation with:

Consumer and Corporate Affairs Canada
Corporations Branch
Place du Portage, 50 Victoria Street
Hull, Quebec
K1A 0C9
Tel: (819) 997-1142
or
Consumer and Corporate Affairs Canada
Bankruptcy and Corporate Services Branch
25 St. Clair Avenue East
7th Floor
Toronto, Ontario
M4T 1M2
Tel: (416) 973-3710

55

Municipal Licences

Many but not all types of businesses require a municipal licence. The fees can vary from a few dollars to a thousand or more, but in most cases the fees are nominal.

In addition, business and industry must conform to zoning and bylaw regulations. Most municipalities have a planning board to designate areas within the municipality for residential, commercial, light industry, heavy industry, noxious industry, green belt or parkland. Construction, reconstruction, alterations or additions to a building require approval of the designs by the building department.

For details of fees and application requirements contact the building department or bylaw officer in the municipality in which the business is located.

Most municipalities require a building permit before alterations or new construction take place. It is extremely important, therefore, that the business check zoning regulations before signing a lease, and obtain the necessary building permit before making alterations or starting new construction.

For regular business licences, check with your municipal licensing board, commission or bylaw officer.

Things to look into before leasing or purchasing premises for which a licence is required:

1. Contact the local municipality to see if the area where the premises are situated permits the intended use.

2. If the zoning permits the intended use, what cost would be involved to meet the Ontario Building Code standards for the type of licence required for:
- washroom facilities;
- fire and exit doors;
- parking facilities;
- sprinkler and alarm systems, etc.

If you intend to lease premises requiring a licence, be sure to include a clause or condition that will void the lease if a licence is not granted.

Also, include a clause to the effect that the landlord shall rectify any building defects that are addressed by the Ontario Building Code, Ontario Fire Code or municipal property standard by-laws within 60 days, thus enabling the lessee to obtain the licence applied for.

All establishments providing accommodation for the general public must be licensed by the province. This includes hotels, motels, tourist resorts and camp grounds.

If no alcoholic beverages are served, the licence is issued by the Ministry of Tourism and Recreation.

Developers who have selected a site conforming to local zoning bylaws must submit plans to the tourism consultant in the nearest Ministry of Tourism and Recreation office. Plans for "hotels" meeting the definition in the building code should be sent to:

Office of the Fire Marshal
Technical, Research and Consulting Services
7 Overlea Blvd.
3rd Floor
Toronto, Ontario
M4H 1A8
Tel: (416) 965-4852

The Ministry of Tourism and Recreation will inform other regulatory bodies involved, and if all requirements are met, will issue a permit. When the tourist establishment is ready to open, a licence will be issued providing there have been no deviations from the original plan. Fees for the tourist establishment licence are $20 annually for residents and $60 annually for non-residents.

Developers who have no specific location in mind should direct their enquiries to:

Tourism and Recreation Operations
Division
Ministry of Tourism and Recreation
77 Bloor Street West
7th Floor
Toronto, Ontario
M7A 2R9
Tel: (416) 965-3475

LIQUOR LICENCES

Developers who propose to operate establishments where alcoholic beverages will be served must first obtain approval from the Liquor Licence Board of Ontario.

A formal application must be made and plans submitted to:

The Liquor Licence Board of Ontario
55 Lake Shore Blvd. East
Toronto, Ontario
M5E 1A4
Tel: (416) 326-0456

IMPORT-EXPORT

In addition to a knowledge of basic business practices, a good knowledge of documentation procedures and the various forms of import-export financing is required.

Persons importing goods into Canada on a regular basis should obtain an importer's number.

Certain products are on a restricted list of imports. There are also items that are exportable only on a quota basis.

The Customs and Excise Division, Revenue Canada, provides a special information service. Anyone contemplating entering the import-export business should first contact the appropriate regional office:

Central Region
Customs and Excise
33 Court Street South
Room 210
Thunder Bay, Ontario
P7B 2W6
Tel: (807) 345-5421

Hamilton Region
10 John Street South
Hamilton, Ontario
L8N 3K7
Tel: (416) 572-2891

London Region
Customs and Excise
451 Talbot Street
TPA Unit
P.O. Box 5940
Terminal "A"
London, Ontario
N6A 4T9
Tel: (519) 645-5843

Ottawa Region
360 Coventry Road
Ottawa, Ontario
K1K 2C6
Tel: (613) 993-0534

Southwestern Ontario Region
Customs and Excise
Federal Building
185 Ouellette Avenue
Windsor, Ontario
N9A 4H8
Tel: (519) 973-8500

Toronto Region
Customs and Excise
Revenue Canada
Customer Services
and Information Unit
1 Front Street West
Toronto, Ontario
M5W 1A3
Tel: (416) 973-8022

Interurban transportation of commodities for compensation requires the carrier to hold an Operating Licence that contains a class of authority allowing the undertaking. Carriers operating entirely within an urban municipality, such as Metropolitan Toronto, are exempt from holding such authority.

Requirements to hold an authority only apply to public trucks and not to passenger automobiles. Some exemptions do apply, such as certain field crops and livestock transported in a truck with not more than three axles, and not towing a trailer.

For commercial vehicles carrying goods for compensation across provincial or international boundaries the carrier will be required to be licensed in Ontario under the Motor Vehicle Transport Act (Canada). They will also be required to be licensed in the other jurisdiction.

Potential carriers should contact either the Carrier Licensing Office or a Ministry Enforcement Office with any questions or concerns regarding the proper class of authority that may be required.

For further information contact:
Carrier Licensing Office
Ministry of Transportation
Main Floor, East Building
1201 Wilson Avenue
Downsview, Ontario
M3M 1J8
Tel: (416) 235-4493
Fax: (416) 235-4363

Manufacturers in bond may, under the authority of the Excise Act, receive into their premises alcohol and other excisable goods at preferred rates of duty when they are for use in the manufacture of products such as proprietary medicines, pharmaceutical preparations, essences and extract, perfumes, vinegar, approved chemical compositions, toilet preparations or cosmetics subject to excise tax. These products are manufactured under government supervision.

An excise bonding warehouse is any approved premises where goods subject to excise may be stored in bond without payment of duty. Goods may be transferred in bond from one bonding warehouse to another or exported in bond without payment of duty. In case of transferral or export, the shipper is liable to any accrued duty until the obligation of the bond is cancelled by the delivery of the goods.

Except in the case of spirits and alcohol, the sale of which is further controlled by provincial liquor boards or commissions, excisable goods are shipped without restriction when duty has been paid. Potable spirit, even when duty has been paid, is shipped only to provincial liquor boards or commissions.

Applications for a licence to manufacture in bond under the Excise Act must be made to the regional director of excise in whose region business is to be carried on. In addition, a guarantee bond must be furnished to Revenue Canada in such sums as may be designated.

SURETY BONDS

A bond is issued by an insurance company and generally guarantees the performance of a contract or compliance with a by-law or statute. It is a three party instrument involving a Principal, an Obligee and a Surety. The Principal is the person performing the contract or applying for the license. The Obligee is the person for whom the work under the contract is performed or the Registrar of the Act. The Surety is the insurance company offering the guarantee.

Surety bonds include contract bonds, license and permit bonds, court and probate bonds, all of which involve a guarantee of performance. Surety bonds give the Obligee the assurance that the Principal is qualified to do the job.

A Fidelity Bond is issued by an insurance company and is designed to pay the Insured for loss resulting from dishonest or fraudulent acts of its employees.

For further information contact your insurance agent or broker or:

Insurance Bureau of Canada
240 Duncan Mill Road
Suite 700
Don Mills, Ontario
M3B 1Z4
Tel: (416) 445-5912.

CHAPTER 4:
SPECIAL REGULATORY LICENCES

Many businesses including retail and service outlets,

restaurants and lounges, manufacturing and processing

operations, may be subject to licences. These licences are

designed to protect the interests and safety of the public

regarding the use, application or sale of certain items or

services. These include food, drugs, alcoholic beverages,

wood products, optical lenses, motor vehicle operations,

railroad and water transportation, pressure vessels and

pressure regulators, and upholstered and stuffed articles.

This list is not all-inclusive, but indicates areas in which special licensing requirements are mandatory.

If your business involves selling products or services to the public, you will need to be aware of the 19 regulatory acts administered by the Business Practices Division of the Ministry of Consumer and Commercial Relations.

Designed primarily to promote fair business practices and a high level of ethical conduct in the marketplace, these 19 acts are designed to protect the rights and needs of the individual consumer. Of particular concern to most businesses is The Business Practices Act.

The Business Practices Act

Referred to as "umbrella legislation", the act has far-reaching implications and powers and applies to many business situations covered by other legislation both within the business practices division and in other ministries and jurisdictions.

Basically, it prohibits and creates sanctions against a wide range of unfair practices and techniques in consumer sales and services. It provides consumers with a right of private redress where it is established that an unfair practice has occurred. There are 22 specific unfair practices prohibited, which fall into two categories - false, misleading or deceptive consumer representations and unconscionable consumer representations.

Each of the following acts is designed to regulate a particular industry. Details regarding registration, bonding and whether or not a written examination is required are outlined below.

Note that each of these acts varies in terms of registration, the control of commercial standards, the inspection of registrants as may be necessary, and the handling of complaints. These acts also empower the ministry to take investigative or enforcement action when required.

The Bailiffs Act

Regulates the appointment and conduct of private bailiffs and the handling of complaints and enquiries regarding the practices of private bailiffs.

Note: Any business using the services of a private bailiff must ensure that the bailiff is duly appointed in the appropriate county or district.

The Consumer Protection Act

Provides for the registration and bonding of itinerant sellers, regulates the use of executory contracts, requires full disclosure of the cost of borrowing, regulates advertising and provides measures for regulating the assignment of contracts and the use of disclaimer clauses.

The Consumer Protection Bureau Act

Outlines the duties of the Consumer Services Bureau, disseminates information for the education of consumers, receives and investigates consumer complaints and enforces legislation enacted in the public interest.

The Consumer Reporting Act

Provides for the registration of consumer reporting agencies and those persons employed in investigating personal information for consumer reporting purposes.

The act requires responsible conduct from businesses and includes a number of specific requirements for gathering and giving out of credit and personal information.

The Collection Agencies Act

Provides for the registration and bonding of collection agencies and branches, the registration of collectors and the administration of written examinations by collection agency owner/operators.

Note: Any business requiring the services of a collection agency is required to deal with a registered agency.

The Motor Vehicle Dealers Act

Provides for the registration of all motor vehicle dealers and for the registration of all sales people. Dealers are required to participate in a compensation fund.

The Motor Vehicle Repair Act

Under this legislation, repair shops must provide written estimates on request, a warranty on new and reconditioned parts and associated labor for a minimum of 90 days or 5,000 km and full disclosure of repair rates to the consumer.

The Paperback And Periodical Distributors Act

Regulates wholesale distributors by requiring them to obtain a licence and be registered before doing business in Ontario. The act also controls the extent of non-resident ownership or control of paperback and periodical distribution systems.

The Prepaid Services Act

This legislation affects fitness, health and martial arts clubs where members pay in advance for services. The legislation limits the length of contracts to one year, provides for a five-day cooling-off period and makes installment payment plans mandatory.

The Real Estate And Business Brokers Act

Provides for the registration of both real estate brokers and sales people and the bonding of brokers, and for written examination prior to registration. The act also regulates trading within Ontario of subdivision lots and condominiums located outside Ontario.

The Travel Industry Act

Regulates persons who are in the business of selling and dealing in travel services. The act provides for registration and bonding of all travel agents and wholesalers. It also requires all registrants to participate in a compensation fund. The fund will be used to protect the consumer in case of bankruptcy or unfulfilled services.

The Cemeteries Act

The Cemeteries Regulation Section regulates operation of all cemeteries, crematoria, mausolea, columbaria and burial grounds. The section also answers inquiries and investigates consumer complaints about cemeteries and burials, and advises cemetery owners. No special legislation exists for monument dealers.

The Funeral Directors and Establishment Act

Protects monies that have been paid to a funeral establishment for a funeral that will take place sometime in the future.

The Condominium Act

Covers condominium ownership and is particularly responsive to consumer needs. It is a self-administering Act and problems that cannot be resolved through persuasion must be resolved by the courts.

The Discriminatory Business Practices Act
Covers discrimination in the business community on the basis of race, creed, colour, nationality, ancestry, place of origin, sex or geographical location.

The Debt Collectors Act
The act prohibits the use of any document giving the appearance it was issued by the courts, if in fact, it was not.

The Theatres Act
The Theatres Section, which administers the amended Theatres Act is responsible for the safety of film theatre-goers in Ontario; the approval for public exhibition and distribution of all 35mm, 16mm and 8mm film and videotape; and the approval of all printed advertising related to the public exhibition of film.

The Athletics Control Act
Responsible for the proper conduct of all professional combative sports in Ontario and issues licences to professional boxers, kickboxers and wrestlers and all officials involved in these sports.

For more detailed information about these acts and others that may relate to business operations, we suggest the following source:

Ministry of Consumer and Commercial Relations
Consumer Information Centre
555 Yonge Street
Toronto, Ontario
M7A 2H6
Tel: (416) 326-8555 or
Toll free 1-800-268-1142 (except area code 807)
Area Code 807, call collect at (416) 326-8555
TDD/TTY (416) 326-8566

Copies of the acts may also be obtained from Publications Ontario, 880 Bay Street, Toronto, Ontario, M7A 1N8.

Enquiries about food, drug, cosmetic, medical devices, and radiation emitting device regulations covered by the Food and Drug Act and Regulations and Radiation Emitting Device Act and Regulations should be directed to the appropriate office listed below.

Health Protection Branch
Health and Welfare Canada
Ontario Offices

Hamilton
150 Main Street West
Room 530
Hamilton, Ontario
L8P 1H8
Tel: (416) 572-2568/9

London
451 Talbot Street
Room 707
London, Ontario
N6A 5C9
Tel: (519) 645-4125

Ontario Regional Office
2301 Midland Avenue
Scarborough, Ontario
M1P 4R7
Tel: (416) 973-1600

Ottawa
Northern/Eastern Ontario
2323 Riverside Drive
SBI Building
11th Floor
Ottawa, Ontario
K1A OL2
Tel: (613) 954-6807

Sudbury
New Federal Building
Room 317
19 Lisgar Street South
Sudbury, Ontario
P3E 3L4
Tel: (705) 671-0606

Consumer and Corporate Affairs Canada
5075 Yonge Street
Suite 202
Willowdale, Ontario
M2N 6C6
Tel: (416) 224-3951

PRODUCT SAFETY

Consumer and Corporate Affairs Canada
Product Safety
200 Town Centre Court
Suite 815
Scarborough, Ontario
M1P 4X8
Tel: (416) 973-4705
or
Consumer and Corporate Affairs Canada
Product Safety
10 John Street South
6th Floor
Hamilton, Ontario
L8N 4A7
Tel: (416) 572-2845

*TECHNICAL
STANDARDS*

Ontario Ministry of Consumer and
Commercial Relations
Technical Standards Division
3300 Bloor Street West
3rd Floor, West Tower
Etobicoke, Ontario
M8X 2X4
   Pressure Vessels Safety Branch
     (416) 234-6000
   Elevating Devices and Special
   Devices Branch
     (416) 234-6060
   Fuels Safety Branch
     (416) 234-6030
   Upholstered and Stuffed Articles Branch
     (416) 234-6088

BUILDING CODE

Ministry of Housing
Ontario Buildings Branch
777 Bay Street
2nd Floor
Toronto, Ontario
M5G 2E5
Tel: (416) 585-6666

POLLUTION CONTROL

The Ministry of the Environment is responsible for the establishment and control of environmental safeguards. Major objectives are the management of water and waste and the development and maintenance of Ontario's natural environment.

For information regarding the control of contaminant emissions, environmental safeguards and the management of air, water and waste, enquire at the regional office or:

Ontario Ministry of the Environment
Communications Branch
135 St. Clair Avenue West
Toronto, Ontario
M4V 1P5
Tel: (416) 323-4663

WEIGHTS AND MEASURES

Under the Weights and Measures Act, most weighing and measuring devices used for trade in Canada must meet certain standards of accuracy.

While federal weights and measures inspectors regularly inspect all weighing and measuring devices in Canada to verify their accuracy, the Weights and Measures Act makes traders legally responsible for the accuracy of their devices.

For further information about the Weights and Measures Act contact your nearest Weights and Measures Office of Consumer and Corporate Affairs Canada.

CHAPTER 5:
TAXATION

Retail Sales Tax

This is a consumption tax based on the retail price of most goods; also taxed are certain services and prices of admission. Most goods and equipment used in a business, other than certain categories of production machinery and materials used in manufacturing, are taxable. Certain purchases such as food products, farm implements and children's clothing are exempt from tax.

The tax rate is 8 percent on most purchases of goods and on labour charges to install, repair and maintain taxable goods and equipment. Tax is also payable at 8 percent on all prepared food products purchased from an eating establishment, where the total charge is more than $4. Liquor, beer and wine sold in restaurants, taverns, etc. are taxable at 10 percent. Tax at 12 percent applies if these items are purchased from retail outlets. Admission to a place of amusement, where the charge is more than $4, is taxable at the rate of 10 percent.

Most lodging, as provided by hotels, motels and lodges, is taxable at 5 percent.

Businesses that sell taxable goods, provide a taxable service or charge admission to a place of amusement must obtain a vendor permit and are responsible for collecting tax and remitting it on a regular basis. There is no fee for this permit.

Further retail sales tax information on vendor permits and exempt purchases may be obtained from the following offices:

71

Retail Sales Tax Offices

Durham
1600 Champlain Avenue
2nd Floor
Whitby, Ontario
L1N 9B2
Tel: (416) 432-3332
Toll free: 1-800-668-5810

Hamilton
119 King Street West
P.O. Box 2112
Hamilton, Ontario
L8N 3Z9
Tel: (416) 521-7504
Toll free: 1-800-263-9229

Kitchener
449 Belmont Avenue West
Kitchener, Ontario
N2M 1N2
Tel: (519) 576-8400
Toll free: 1-800-265-2587

London
Westminster Centre
334 Wellington Road South
Unit 1
London, Ontario
N6C 4P6
Tel: (519) 433-3901
Toll free: 1-800-265-1540

North Bay
Northgate Plaza
1500 Fisher Street
North Bay, Ontario
P1B 2H3
Tel: (705) 474-4900
Toll free: 1-800-461-1564

Ottawa
1355 Bank Street
3rd Floor
Ottawa, Ontario
K1H 8K7
Tel: (613) 523-9760
Toll free: 1-800-267-9745

Peel
2 Robert Speck Parkway
Suite 350
Mississauga, Ontario
L4Z 1H8
Tel: (416) 273-9490
Toll free: 1-800-268-2968

Toronto
2300 Yonge Street
10th Floor
Toronto, Ontario
M4P 1H6
Tel: (416) 487-1361
Toll free:
1-800-268-8852

Ministry of Revenue Information Offices

Barrie
109 Ferris Lane
Barrie, Ontario
L4M 2Y1
Tel: (705) 739-1511
Toll free: 1-800-267-7968

Belleville
191 Dundas Street East
Belleville, Ontario
K8N 1E2
Tel: (613) 962-9108
Zenith 37100

Sudbury
Ontario Government
Building
199 Larch Street
Sudbury, Ontario
P3E 5P9
Tel: (705) 675-4351
Toll free: 1-800-461-1564

Windsor
Ontario Government
Building
250 Windsor Avenue
Windsor, Ontario
N9A 6V9
Tel: (519) 252-4404
Toll free: 1-800-265-1540

Thunder Bay
Revenue Information
Centre
Victoriaville Mall
Unit 5
700 Victoria Avenue East
Thunder Bay, Ontario
P7C 5P7
Tel: (807) 475-1681
Toll free: 1-800-465-5025

Corporations Tax

Corporations tax is levied and collected by the province under the authority of the Ontario Corporations Tax Act. It comprises two elements: income tax, which is levied on taxable income, and capital tax, which is levied on taxable paid-up capital. For both taxes, there are preferential rates for small businesses. The rates are as follows:

Income Tax

The general rate is 15.5 percent but the effective rate is 10 percent on active business income that qualifies for the federal small business deduction.

Capital Tax

The general rate is .3 percent but the flat rates for small businesses are:

$0 (i.e. an exemption) for corporations with both total assets and gross revenue of $1 million or less.

$100 for corporations with total assets or gross revenues over $1 million, but with taxable capital up to $1 million.

$200 for corporations with total assets or gross revenues over $1 million, but both not over $1.5 million, and taxable capital exceeding $1 million but not exceeding $2 million.

$500 for corporations with total assets or gross revenue in excess of $1.5 million, and taxable capital in excess of $1 million but not over $2 million.

$100 for family farm/fishing corporations; mortgage investment corporations; credit unions and mutual insurance corporations insuring churches, schools and charitable organizations if they do not qualify for the capital tax exemption.

Each corporation that is liable to pay the tax should file an Ontario Corporations Tax Return (CT 23) within six months after its taxation year end. When total tax exceeds $2,000, payments are made monthly; in other cases payments are made annually.

For further information, contact:
Ministry of Revenue
Corporations Tax Branch
P.O Box 622
33 King Street West
Oshawa, Ontario
L1H 8H6
1 (800) 263-7965

Gasoline Tax

Ontario levies a direct tax on every retail sale of gasoline. This tax is collected by service stations or other retailers from their customers and is remitted through their suppliers. No registration by the retailer is required for gasoline.

Fuel Tax

Ontario levies a direct tax on every retail sale of clear middle distillate fuel. This tax is collected by retailers from their customers and is remitted through their suppliers.

Untaxed middle distillate fuel is coloured (red) for non-taxable uses. (e.g. heating, cooking or generating power in unlicensed equipment used for commercial, industrial or institutional purposes.) The use of coloured fuel in a licensed motor vehicle or in unlicensed recreation equipment is prohibited.

Operators of diesel-powered commercial motor vehicles travelling into or out of Ontario are required to obtain and place on their motor vehicles a Fuel Tax Registration decal issued by the Motor Fuels and Tobacco Tax Branch.

Tobacco Tax

Persons retailing cigarettes and other tobacco products must hold a valid vendor's permit issued under The Retail Sales Tax Act. The tobacco tax, which they are required to collect on their sales of tobacco products, is remitted through their wholesale supplier, who may be appointed as a collector. Retailers must ensure that their wholesale supplier holds a wholesale dealer's permit as there are penalties for purchasing tobacco products from non-collectors. In addition, retailers will collect and remit 8 percent retail sales tax on all tobacco products sold.

Persons selling cigarettes and other tobacco products for resale are deemed wholesalers and may hold a wholesale dealer's permit. They must also be designated as collectors. There is no fee for the wholesale dealer's permit or the collector designation.

Effective November 1, 1990 when Ontario's Cigarette Marking Program is fully implemented, the stocking or selling of cigarettes that do not bear an Ontario tax mark is prohibited. Unauthorized possession of unmarked cigarettes will result in heavy fines in addition to the forfeiture of the product.

Permits - Fuel and Tobacco

Details on registration, wholesale dealers' permits and designation as a collector for tobacco tax, may be obtained from:

Ministry of Revenue
Motor Fuels and Tobacco Tax Branch
P.O. Box 627
33 King Street West
Oshawa, Ontario
L1H 8H5
Tel: (416) 433-6389 - Fuel Tax
     (416) 433-6394 - Tobacco Tax

Land Transfer Tax

Every individual or corporation obtaining an interest in land in Ontario is liable to Land Transfer Tax. The tax is based on the consideration of all lands, buildings, estates, rights, or interests in them, including options and long-term leases.

An exemption from Land Transfer Tax may be available where the transfer of land is from an individual to his or her family farm corporation or family business corporation. Retail sales tax may still be payable when chattels associated with the land are transferred. Contact your local retail sales tax office for further information, or contact:

Ministry of Revenue
Motor Fuels and Tobacco Tax Branch
33 King Street West
Oshawa, Ontario
L1H 8H9
Tel: (416) 433-6360

Goods and Services Tax

The Goods and Services Tax (GST) replaced the Federal Sales Tax (FST) on January 1, 1991. The majority of goods and services sold or provided in Canada are subject to the GST currently at 7 percent.

There are some goods and services such as basic groceries or exports which are *zero-rated*. In addition, a limited number of goods and services, such as certain health care or financial services, are exempt from the GST.

Registration Under GST

Every business or organization engaged in a commercial activity with annual sales and revenues of GST taxable goods and services of more than $30,000 is required to be registered.

Input Tax Credits

Businesses that are registered for the GST are able to claim a credit (referred to as an input tax credit) for the GST paid or payable on business purchases. The credit is applied against the GST charged on sales to determine whether tax should be remitted or a refund claimed.

Excise Taxes

Most of the existing excise taxes imposed under the Excise Tax Act remain in effect since the implementation of the GST. If both excise tax and the GST are applicable, the excise tax is applied *before* the GST.

Examples of some goods subject to excise tax at specific rates are the following:

- Jewellery...10 percent
- Automotive air conditioners...$100
- Unleaded gasoline...$0.85 per litre

Additional information about federal commodity taxes may be obtained from your local District Offices. Please refer to the blue pages of your telephone directory for the telephone numbers that are not available at the time of this printing. The following publications available from Revenue Canada have been specifically written for small businesses. Please write to your District Office for a copy.

- "GST Guide for Small Business"
- "Simplified Accounting Methods for Small Businesses"

Regional Offices

Ottawa Region
Ottawa District Office
1730 St. Laurent Blvd.
P.O. Box 8257
Ottawa, Ontario
K1G 3H7

North Bay
North Bay District Office
P.O. Box 477
North Bay, Ontario
P1B 8J2

Kingston
Kingston District Office
993 Princess Street
Kingston, Ontario
K7L 1H3

Toronto Region
Toronto East District Office
305 Milner Avenue
4th Floor
Scarborough, Ontario
M1B 3V4

Toronto West District Office
90 Burnhamthorpe Road
West
3rd Floor
Mississauga, Ontario
L5B 3C3

Toronto Core District Office
375 University Avenue
9th Floor
Toronto, Ontario
M5C 2J5

Toronto North District
Office
4576 Yonge Street
7th Floor
North York, Ontario
M2N 6N5

Barrie
Barrie District Office
1st Floor, 99 Ferris Lane
Barrie, Ontario
L4M 2Y2

Hamilton
Hamilton District Office
3rd Floor, 120 King St.
West
P.O. Box 588
Postal Station A
Hamilton, Ontario
LBN 3K7

Southwestern Region
London District Office
5th Floor, 148 Fullarton
Street
P.O. Box 638
Postal Station B
London, Ontario
N6A 4Y4

St. Catharines
St. Catharines District
Office
2nd Floor, 1 St. Paul Street
Tower Building
St. Catharines, Ontario
L2R 7L4

Windsor
Windsor District Office
2nd Floor, 215 Eugenie
Street, West
P.O. Box 360
Postal Station A
Windsor, Ontario
N8X 2X7

Waterloo
Waterloo District Office
1st Floor, Lutheran Life
Bldg.
470 Weber Street North
P.O. Box 1617
Waterloo, Ontario
N2J 4T4

Thunder Bay
Thunder Bay District Office
300-214 Red River Road
Thunder Bay, Ontario
P7B 1A6

Sault St. Marie/
Sudbury/Kirkland Lake
Offices: FST Rebate appli-
cation to be mailed to the
North Bay District Office at
the address noted above.

Federal Corporations Tax

Corporations are required to remit their federal tax, in monthly installments, to Revenue Canada. An Income Tax return is due six months after the corporation's year end. (Also see Source Deductions)

Personal Tax

All persons resident in Canada are subject to the requirements of the Income Tax Act and may be required to pay income tax on their world income. Federal and provincial tax are paid together on the personal Income Tax return. This return is due April 30 of the following year. Quarterly installments of income tax are required under some circumstances.

Sole proprietorship and partnership income is included on the individual tax return and taxed at the normal rates.

Capital Gains Tax

Only a portion of capital gains or losses are included in income; the amount to be included depends upon the tax year. Losses may only be used to reduce the amount of any gain to nil. Any excess may be applied against gains of other years. Personal residences are exempt from the capital gains tax.

Source Deductions

Businesses are required to remit the amount of Canada Pension Plan contributions, Unemployment Insurance contributions and Income Tax up to 4 times a month. The frequency of the remittance depends upon the pay period and the amount remitted.

Further information on Income Tax requirements is available, by phone or in person, from Revenue Canada's District Taxation Offices.

Revenue Canada - District Taxation Offices

Belleville
11 Station Street
Belleville, Ontario
K8N 2S3
Tel: (613) 969-3706

Hamilton
150 Main Street West
Hamilton, Ontario
L8N 3E1
Tel: (416) 522-8671

Kingston
385 Princess Street
Kingston, Ontario
K7L 1C1
Tel: (613) 545-8371

Kitchener
166 Frederick Street
Kitchener, Ontario
N2G 4N1
Tel: (519) 579-2230

London
451 Talbot Street
London, Ontario
N6A 5E5
Tel: (519) 645-4211

Mississauga
P.O. Box 6000
77 City Centre Drive
Mississauga, Ontario
L5A 4E9
Tel: (416) 566-6700

North York
P.O. Box 7057
36 Adelaide Street East
Toronto, Ontario
M5C 2V4
Tel: (416) 869-1500

Ottawa
360 Lisgar Street
Ottawa, Ontario
K1A 0L9
Tel: (613) 598-2275

Scarborough
200 Town Center Court
Scarborough, Ontario
M1P 4Y3
Tel: (416) 296-1950

St. Catharines
P.O. Box 3038
32 Church Street
St. Catharines, Ontario
L2R 6R4
Tel: (416) 688-4000

Sudbury
19 Lisgar Street South
Sudbury, Ontario
P3E 3L5
Tel: (705) 671-0581

Thunder Bay
201 North May Street
Thunder Bay, Ontario
P7C 3P5
Tel: (807) 623-3443

Toronto
36 Adelaide Street East
Toronto, Ontario
M5C 1J7
Tel: (416) 869-1500

Windsor
185 Ouellette Avenue
Windsor, Ontario
N9A 5S8
Tel: (519) 258-8302

CHAPTER 6:
PATENTS, TRADE-MARKS, INDUSTRIAL DESIGNS, COPYRIGHTS

A patent is a document issued by the Government of

Canada, by the Canadian Patent Office, giving a patentee

the right to exclude others from making, using or selling

his or her invention.

PATENTS

Under the Patent Act, as amended in 1989, a patent comes into force when granted by the Commissioner of Patents; it expires 20 years after first filing of the application in Canada. Some protection starts when the application is published by the Patent Office, 18 months after filing. Patent protection cannot be extended past the 20-year period.

Protection of patentable inventions in other countries can only be obtained by obtaining patents in those countries. By the same token, foreign patents do not protect inventions in Canada.

Persons interested in obtaining a patent should consult a qualified registered patent agent because the process is complex. Improperly prepared documentation can result in delays and a weak patent.

In addition, patent agents can advise their clients whether they are likely to be able to receive a patent and suggest patenting strategies. Patent agents are experts in conducting patent searches.

Patent applications should be made as early as possible. In Canada, patents will not be granted if they have been made public or described before filing. The one exception is a disclosure made by the applicant or someone who obtained information from the applicant less than a year before filing. Even that exception, however, can fail. Most foreign countries also reject applications after public disclosure. Inventions should not be used publicly or offered for sale prior to filing, for the same reasons.

Once issued, a patent may be assigned (the rights may be sold), or the manufacturing licensed by the inventor.

The Patent Office does not assist inventors in the development or marketing of inventions. The Patent Office is also prohibited from expressing an opinion on the patentability of an invention until a formal application has been filed.

The protection of rights under a patent is the responsibility of the patent holder. The Patent Office does not defend a patent holder charged with infringement, nor will it prosecute others who infringe the patent holder's rights.

The average time from the filing of an application to the granting of a patent is about three years. The fees are as follows:

- on filing application for patent, $150 for small entities and $300 for others;
- for grant of patent, $350 for small entities and $700 for others plus $4 per page for each page in excess of 100 pages.

Patent Pending

The patent pending marking offers no positive protection. However, it does warn other manufacturers who may be contemplating copying a product that an application for patent has been filed.

Where costly tooling or marketing expenses are involved, this is frequently enough to discourage competitors. On the other hand, it is an open admission that the product in question does not have patent protection.

The address of the Patent Office is:

The Patent Office
Consumer & Corporate Affairs Canada
Place du Portage, Tower 1
50 Victoria Street
Hull, Quebec
K1A 0E1
Tel: (819) 997-1936

A trade-mark in most instances is a word, symbol or design, or a combination of these, used to distinguish the goods or services of a person, organization or corporation in the marketplace from those of others.

From a business point of view it is an extremely valuable marketing device and is generally defended to the full extent of the law.

From the consumer's point of view it serves to eliminate confusion and establish the origin and consistency of quality of the product or service under consideration.

The registration of trade-marks is not mandatory, but is advisable because it provides evidence of ownership and is, therefore, more easily defended. It should be noted that defence of the trade-mark is the responsibility of the owner, not the Trade-marks Office.

Trade-marks are valid for a period of 15 years from date of registration, at which time they may be renewed on application and payment of a $300 fee.

Renewals may be issued every 15 years without limitation. Trade-marks are valid only in the country in which they are issued; it is, therefore, necessary to register in countries to which exports are planned if the mark is to be protected abroad.

Individuals may prepare their own application or work through a registered trade-mark agent. It normally takes about a year from date of application to registration if no opposition or other obstacles intervene.

Trade-marks may be assigned or sold, but all such changes must be registered with the Registrar of Trade-marks.

The fee for filing an application for registration of a trade-mark is $150. The fee for the issuance of a certificate of registration of a trade-mark is $200.

Trade Name

A trade name is the name under which a business is operated. A trade name can be registered under the Trade-marks Act only if it also serves as a trade-mark.

Quality Mark/Hallmark

A quality mark indicates the quality, quantity, fineness, weight, thickness, proportion or kind of precious metal in an article.

Precious metal articles are made from gold, silver, platinum or palladium.

Most precious metal articles do not have to be quality marked, but if a quality mark is applied, it must also carry a registered trade-mark or acceptable foreign hallmark.

A hallmark is a mark indicating the quality of a precious metal applied by a foreign country with recognized standards.

Compulsory marking is required for most hollowware, some gold plated spectacle frames and some plated flatware.

Timber Mark

A timber mark is a special mark used by persons engaged in lumbering to identify ownership of logs floated or rafted on inland waters within Ontario, Quebec and New Brunswick. A timber mark is registered with the Copyright Office. The fee is $2.00, and there is no limit to its term.

For more detailed information, consult your attorney or trade-mark agent. Copies of the Trade-marks Act and the Trade-marks Rules are available from:

Supply and Service Canada
Publishing Centre
Hull, Quebec
K1A 0S9
Tel: (819) 997-2560

Enquiries concerning the Precious Metals Act may be directed to (819) 997-1177 in Hull, Quebec, or to your district office, Consumer and Corporate Affairs Canada.

INDUSTRIAL DESIGNS

An industrial design is any original shape, pattern or ornamentation applied to a useful article of manufacture that is mass produced. The article can be made by hand, tool or machine.

The protection offered is for an initial period of five years and is valid only in Canada. Initial registration fee is $160. A renewal may be obtained for a further five years for a fee of $215.

Registration must be completed within 12 months after the design has been made public in Canada.

Only the author of the design may obtain registration, unless the author was hired to create the design, in which case the employer is the owner, and the only one authorized to request registration.

Industrial designs may be sold outright or may be licensed. Such transactions should be recorded with the Industrial Design Office.

Protection provided by the Industrial Design Act is frequently confused with protection under the Copyright Act. However, once the original artistic work is used or intended to be used as a model or pattern to produce more than 50 single useful articles or sets of useful articles, the artistic work then becomes an industrial design, which can only be protected under the Industrial Design Act.

Registration normally takes about 8 to 10 months unless changes to descriptions or drawings are required. The Industrial Design Office is not permitted to express opinions on the merits of a design or indicate whether the design is acceptable prior to the submission of a formal application.

While it is possible for the individual to proceed alone, it is advisable to obtain the services of a registered patent agent or attorney.

Further information may be obtained by contacting:

The Copyright and Industrial Design Branch
Consumer and Corporate Affairs Canada
Ottawa-Hull
K1A 0C9
Tel: (819) 997-1725
The Industrial Design Office is located at:
Place du Portage I, Phase I
50 Victoria Street
Hull, Quebec
K1A 0C9

COPYRIGHTS

The owner of the copyright, who is normally the author or creator, is the only person who may copy or permit someone else to copy the work. Copying includes publishing, producing, reproducing or performing.

In Canada, copyright is automatically acquired upon creation of an original work provided that, at the time, the author is one of the following:

- a Canadian citizen or a British subject;
- a resident within the British commonwealth;
- a citizen or subject of a country belonging to the Berne Copyright Convention;
- a citizen or subject of a country with which Canada has a reciprocal arrangement.

Although it is not necessary to register a copyright, registration is evidence that the person registered is the copyright owner. Registration can also be used in court to establish ownership.

Authors are the first owners of the copyrights to their work unless they were hired to create the work, in which case the employer is the copyright owner.

Copyright applies to all original literary, dramatic, musical and artistic works. These include books, writings, musical works, sculptures, paintings, photographs, motion pictures, dictionaries, encyclopedias and computer programs. Copyright also applies to mechanical and electronic contrivances such as records, audio tapes and cassettes and compact discs.

In Canada, the duration of the copyright is for the life of the author plus 50 years, except where:

<u>Author unknown</u>: Copyright exists for 50 years from the date of first publication of the work.

<u>Crown copyright</u>: Copyright in a work published by or under the direction of Her Majesty the Queen or any government department exists for 50 years from the date of first publication of the work.

<u>Mechanical or electronic contrivances</u> (records, tapes and other contrivances by means of which sounds may be mechanically or electronically reproduced): The term of copyright is for 50 years from the date of making the original plate or tape from which the contrivance was directly or indirectly derived.

<u>Photographs</u>: Copyright exists for 50 years from the date of making the original negative from which the photograph was directly or indirectly derived.

<u>Posthumous works</u>: For works not published at the time of the author's death, copyright exists for 50 years from the date of their publication, delivery or performance.

Works of joint authorship: Copyright exists during the life of the author who dies last and 50 years following that author's death.

Canadian copyrights are valid in all countries that are members of either the Berne Copyright Convention or the Universal Copyright Convention, which includes most of the countries in the world, the notable exception being China.

The provisions of the Universal Copyright Convention require that all copies of works, from the time of first publication, be marked with a small c in a circle, the name of the copyright owner, and the year of first publication (for example © J. Smith 1985).

Copyrights may be sold or licensed and reproduction rights, film rights, translation rights, performance rights may be negotiated separately. Rights may also be sold on a geographic basis, with the rights to a work being held by one person in Australia, by another in Britain and still another in the United States - all at the same time.

The fee for examination and registration of a copyright is $35 (subject to change without notice). A certificate is issued when the application is approved.

On the death of a copyright holder, the copyright becomes part of the estate and the property of the heirs. Copyrights may also be issued to the heirs for works unregistered prior to the author's death.

Copies of the Copyright Act and rules are available at any bookstore selling federal government publications or from:

Supply and Services Canada
Publishing Centre
Mail Order Section
Hull, Quebec
K1A 0S9

The mailing address of the Canadian Copyright Office is:

Copyright and Industrial Design Branch
Bureau of Corporate Affairs
Consumer and Corporate Affairs Canada
Ottawa, Ontario
K1A 0C9

Performing Rights Societies

Royalties paid for public performances of copyrighted musical works are collected by performing rights societies and distributed to their members, the composers, authors or publishers.

These societies are authorized under the Copyright Act to perform this service. The Canadian society is:

Society of Composers, Authors and Music
Publishers of Canada (SOCAN)
41 Valleybrook Drive
Don Mills, Ontario
M3B 2S6
Tel: (416) 445-8700

Society of Composers, Authors and Music
Publishers of Canada (SOCAN)
1240 Bay Street
9th Floor
Toronto, Ontario
M5R 2C2
Tel: (416) 924-4427

CHAPTER 7:
CERTIFICATION

Certification/approval is required on electrical apparatus,

pressure vessels, pressure regulators, gas appliances,

industrial buildings, commercial buildings, farm buildings,

residential buildings, alterations to buildings, electrical

wiring, electrical panels, electrical control systems, plumb-

ing equipment, plumbing installations, plumbing hookups

to external systems and a wide range of other consumer,

commercial, industrial and scientific products.

REGULATORY BODIES

Regulatory bodies generally have arrangements with similar foreign agencies and international standards organizations.

Enquire at:
Canadian Standards Association
178 Rexdale Blvd.
Rexdale, Ontario
M9W 1R3
Tel: (416) 747-4000

Underwriter Laboratories of Canada
7 Crouse Road
Scarborough, Ontario
M1R 3A9
Tel: (416) 757-3611

Canadian Gas Association
55 Scarsdale Road
Don Mills, Ontario
M3B 2R3
Tel: (416) 447-6465

All electrical wiring installations, whether residential, commercial or industrial, must be approved by Hydro inspectors.

In addition, Hydro may issue special inspection approval for custom equipment not in regular manufacture, limited quantity production, imported machine tools or other equipment intended for in-plant use but not for resale, and special situations where it is not practical to submit the equipment for regular C.S.A. approval.

Enquiries should be directed to the Ontario Hydro inspection office in your area or to:

Ontario Hydro
Electrical Inspection Department
700 University Avenue
Toronto, Ontario
M5G 1X6
Tel: (416) 592-3721

Trade certification prevents unqualified persons from working at certain skilled occupations which provides protection and confidence for the public.

Compulsory Certification

Compulsory certification means that only persons holding a Certificate of Qualification or are registered apprentices are permitted to work in the skilled occupation unless exempted by the regulation. These skilled occupations are:

Alignment and brakes mechanic
Auto body repair
Barber
Construction maintenance electrician
Domestic and rural electrician
Fuel and electrical systems mechanic
Hairdresser
Hairstylist
Hoisting engineer - tower crane
Hoisting engineer - mobile crane
Motorcycle mechanic
Motor vehicle mechanic
Plumber
Refrigeration and air conditioning mechanic

Sheet metal worker
Steam fitter
Transmission mechanic
Truck-trailer repairer
Watch repairer

Voluntary Certification
In some skilled occupations, tradespeople may obtain a Certificate of Qualification if they serve an apprenticeship or can show proof of training and/or experience and pass the required examination. However, it is not mandatory to have a certificate to practise the occupation. The trades in this category are:

Assistant cook 1
Automatic machinist
Automotive painter
Baker 2
Baker-patissier
Boat motor mechanic
Brick and stone mason
Cement mason
Construction boilermaker
Construction lineman
Construction millwright
Cook 2
Dry cleaner
Farm equipment mechanic
Fitter (structural/platework)
General carpenter
General machinist
Glazier and metal mechanic
Heavy duty equipment mechanic
Horticulturist - nursery greenhouse worker
Horticulturist - landscape greenskeeper
Industrial electrician
Industrial mechanic (millwright)
Industrial painter
Industrial woodworker
Ironworker
Junior baker 1
Lather

Marine and small powered equipment mechanic
Mold maker
Plasterer
Power lineman
Printer - Letterpress   - job shop
          Lithography - job shop
          Offset press - plant
          Linotype operator
          Compositor
          Pressman   - letterpress
          Compositor   - typesetting,
                          photo typesetting
          Compositor & camera technician
Radio and television service technician
Small engine mechanic
Small engine mechanic (construction)
Sprinkler and fire protection installer
Tool and die maker

The value of this certificate is that it proves recipients are qualified in their trades to Ministry of Skills Development standards.
Contact:
Ministry of Skills Development
Apprenticeship & Client Services Branch
625 Church Street
5th Floor
Toronto, Ontario
M4Y 2E8
Tel: (416) 326-5605

CHAPTER 8:
LABOUR REGULATIONS

Standards for employment and occupational health and

safety are established and controlled by the Ministry of

Labour, which administers and enforces the Employment

Agencies Act, the Employment Standards Act, and the

Occupational Health and Safety Act. The Ministry is also

responsible for the Centre for Disability and Work.

Reporting to the Minister of Labour are: The Pay Equity

Commissioner and The Workers Compensation Board.

For information regarding occupational health and safety,
minimum wage, working hours and so on, enquire at:

> The Ontario Ministry of Labour
> Communications Branch
> 15th Floor
> 400 University Avenue
> Toronto, Ontario
> M7A 1T7
> Tel: (416) 326-7400
>
> Employment Standards Branch
>   (416) 326-7000
>   or Toll free 1-800-387-2965
> Employment Adjustment Branch
>   (416) 326-7381
> Industrial Health and Safety Branch
>   (416) 326-7900
> Construction Health and Safety Branch
>   (416) 326-7770

Mining Health and Safety Branch
(705) 670-7400
Health and Safety
Support Services Branch
(416) 326-1400
Worker's Compensation Board,
Occupational Health
& Safety Education
Authority
(416) 975-9728

Advice on occupational health and safety is also available from occupational health and safety resource centres located at:

University of Waterloo, Waterloo,
Ontario N2L 3G1
Lakehead University, Thunder Bay,
Ontario P7B 5E1
Queen's University, Kingston,
Ontario K7L 2N6
University of Western Ontario, London
Ontario N6A 5B9
Cambrian College
Sudbury, Ontario P3A 3V8

EMPLOYMENT STANDARDS

The Employment Standards Act applies to most employees and employers in the province of Ontario. There are certain exceptions, and these area covered in detail in a pamphlet, "A Guide to the Employment Standards Act", available from the Ontario Ministry of Labour, Communications Branch. The pamphlet also outlines:
- who is covered by the Act and its general application;
- hours of work;
- minimum wage;
- homeworkers;
- public holidays;
- overtime pay;
- vacation pay;
- equal pay for equal work;
- benefit plans;
- pregnancy leave and parental leave;

- termination of employment;
- severance pay;
- payments on termination
- agricultural workers;
- domestics;
- lie detectors;
- retail business establishments;
- general administration.

MINIMUM WAGE

General hourly rate: $5.40
Hourly rate for persons employed to serve liquor in
licensed premises: $4.90
Student, hourly rate. This rate applies to students
under 18 who work 28 hours per week or less during
the school term and more or less than 28 hours per
week during school holidays. $4.55

Rates effective the work week in which October, 1, 1990 occurs;
subject to revision.

VACATION PAY

After one year of service, employees are entitled to two
weeks vacation with pay. The vacation pay must be at
least 4 percent of the total wages for the year for which the
vacation is given.

An employee who terminates before com-
pleting one year of employment must receive 4 percent of
total wages calculated from the first day employed.

The employer shall decide when the vaca-
tion is given. It may be a two-week period or two periods of
one week each. The two weeks vacation must be given
within 10 months after the employee has earned it.

The employee's vacation pay entitlement
must be paid within one week of termination of employment.

Vacation pay benefits apply to full-time,
part-time and student employees.

EQUAL PAY

No employer or person acting on behalf of an employer
shall differentiate between male and female employees by
paying a female employee at a rate of pay less than the
rate of pay paid to a male employee, or vice versa, for sub-

95

stantially the same kind of work performed in the same establishment, the performance of which requires substantially the same skill, effort and responsibility and which is performed under similar working conditions, except where such payment is made pursuant to:

- a seniority system;
- a merit system;
- a system that measures earnings by quantity or quality of production; or
- a differential based on any factor other than sex.

Additional information may be obtained from Employment Standards Branch, Ontario Ministry of Labour, in the following cities:

Hamilton
119 King Street West
Hamilton, Ontario
L8N 3Z9
Tel: (416) 521-7736

Kenora
808 Robertson Street
Kenora, Ontario
P9N 1X9
Tel: (807) 468-2712

Kingston
1055 Princess Street
Kingston, Ontario
K7L 1H3
Tel: (613) 545-4340

Kitchener
824 King Street West
Kitchener, Ontario
N2G 1G1
Tel: (519) 744-8101

London
205 Oxford Street East
2nd Floor
London, Ontario
N6A 5G6
Tel: (519) 439-3231

Mississauga
2 Robert Speck Parkway
Mississauga, Ontario
L4Z 1H8
Tel: (416) 273-7800

Ottawa
2197 Riverside Drive
3rd Floor
Ottawa, Ontario
K1H 7X3
Tel: (613) 523-7530

Sault St. Marie
390 Bay Street
Sault Ste. Marie, Ontario
P6A 1X2
Tel: (705) 949-3331

Scarborough
2500 Lawrence Ave. East
Scarborough, Ontario
M1P 2R7
Tel: (416) 750-3557

St. Catharines
205 King Street
St. Catharines, Ontario
L2R 3J5
Tel: (416) 682-7261

Sudbury
199 Larch Street
Sudbury, Ontario
P3E 5P9
Tel: (705) 675-4455

Thunder Bay
435 James Street South
Thunder Bay, Ontario
P7E 6E3
Tel: (807) 475-1691

Timmins
273 Third Avenue
Timmins, Ontario
P4N 1E2
Tel: (705) 267-6231

Toronto
40 Dundas Street West
4th Floor, Tower B
Toronto, Ontario
M5G 2C2
Tel: (416) 326-7160

Windsor
500 Ouellette Avenue
Windsor, Ontario
N9A 1B3
Tel: (519) 256-8278

SOURCE DEDUCTIONS

Businesses are required to remit the amount of Canada Pension Plan contributions, Unemployment Insurance contributions and Income Tax up to four times a month. The frequency of the remittance depends upon the pay period and the amount remitted.

Further information is available, by phone or in person, from Revenue Canada's District Taxation Offices.

• Revenue Canada

Belleville
11 Station Street
Belleville, Ontario
K8N 2S3
Tel: (613) 962-8611

Hamilton
150 Main Street West
Hamilton, Ontario
L8N 3E1
Tel: (416) 522-8671

Kingston
385 Princess Street
Kingston, Ontario
K7L 1C1
Tel: (613) 545-8371

Kitchener
166 Frederick Street
Kitchener, Ontario
N2G 4N1
Tel: (519) 579-2230

London
451 Talbot Street
London, Ontario
N6A 5E5
Tel: (519) 645-4211

Mississauga
P.O. Box 6000
77 City Centre Drive
Mississauga, Ontario
L5A 4E9
Tel: (416) 869-1500

North York
P.O. Box 7057
36 Adelaide Street East
Toronto, Ontario
M5C 2V4
Tel: (416) 869-1500

Ottawa
360 Lisgar Street
Ottawa, Ontario
K1A 0L9
Tel: (613) 598-2275

Scarborough
200 Town Center Court
Scarborough, Ontario
M1P 4Y3
Tel: (416) 296-1950

St. Catharines
P.O. Box 38
32 Church Street
St. Catharines, Ontario
L2R 6R4
Tel: (416) 688-4000

Sudbury
19 Lisgar Street South
Sudbury, Ontario
P3E 3L5
Tel: (705) 671-0581

Thunder Bay
201 North May Street
Thunder Bay, Ontario
P7C 3P5
Tel: (807) 623-3443

Toronto
36 Adelaide Street East
Toronto, Ontario
M5C 1J7
Tel: (416) 869-1500

Windsor
185 Ouellette Avenue
Windsor, Ontario
N9A 5S8
Tel: (519) 258-8302

The Source Deductions Unit has a complete kit of information for new business people and welcomes the opportunity to discuss and explain the regulations. No appointments are necessary.

Most employers in Ontario are required, by law, to register with the Workers' Compensation Board (WCB) within 30 days of hiring someone.

The WCB compensates workers who are injured on the job or who contract an occupational disease. The Board also covers the costs of medical treatment and rehabilitation. New businesses supply the Board with details about the kind of work their workers will be doing. The business is then classified into a rate group and assessed based on the estimated payroll for the first year of operation. Each year after that, the payroll is estimated for the coming year, while the actual payroll for the past year is recorded.

Sole proprietors, partners and executive officers are not automatically covered by workers' compensation. However, it can be applied for on a voluntary basis.

If you're a new employer, please contact the Worker's Compensation Board immediately. The Board will provide a registration kit which includes information on assessments, coverage, accident reporting and objecting to a WCB decision. The Board also produces several brochures and videos to help explain the compensation system. Contact us at any of the following offices:

Toronto Head Office
Workers'
Compensation Board
2 Bloor Street East
34th Floor
Toronto, Ontario
M4W 3C3
Tel: (416) 927-3925

Hamilton
120 King Street West
Hamilton, Ontario
L8P 4V2
Tel: (416) 523-1800

Kingston
234 Concession Street
Suite 304
Kingston, Ontario
K7L 5T3
Tel: (613) 544-9682

Kitchener/Waterloo
151 Frederick Street
Kitchener, Ontario
N2H 2M2
Tel: (519) 576-4130

London
148 Fullarton Street
London, Ontario
N6A 5P3
Tel: (519) 663-2331

North Bay
128 McIntyre Street West
North Bay, Ontario
P1B 2Y6
Tel: (705) 472-5200

Ottawa
360 Albert Street
Suite 200
Ottawa, Ontario
K1R 7X7
Tel: (613) 238-7851

Sault St. Marie
369 Queen Street East
Suite 101
Sault St. Marie, Ontario
P6A 1Z4
Tel: (705) 942-3002

St. Catharines
Lake-Carlton Plaza
161 Carlton Street
Suite 201
St. Catharines, Ontario
L2R 1R5
Tel: (416) 687-8622

Sudbury
30 Cedar Street
Sudbury, Ontario
P3E 1A4
Tel: (705) 675-9301

Thunder Bay
P.O. Box 7000
410 Memorial Avenue
Thunder Bay, Ontario
P7C 5S2
Tel: (807) 343-1710

Timmins
Hollinger Court
100 Waterloo Road
Timmins, Ontario
P4N 4X5
Tel: (705) 267-6427

Windsor
235 Eugenie Street West
Windsor, Ontario
N8X 2X7
Tel: (519) 966-0660

Long-distance callers may contact Board offices serving their area free of charge. For toll-free numbers, consult your local telephone directory.

OCCUPATIONAL HEALTH

The Occupational Health and Safety Act applies to all workers and work places in the province of Ontario with a few exceptions. The legislation covers:
- the general applicability of the Act;
- the responsibilities of employers, supervisors, workers and suppliers with regard to occupational health and safety;
- the establishment of joint labour and management health and safety committees;

- the control of the exposure of workers to toxic substances;
- refusals to work where health or safety is in danger;
- notification of accidents.

The Act was recently amended by Bill 208 which created an Occupational Health and Safety Agency for training, education, research and consultation. It also increased the number of businesses that require Health and Safety Committees and raised fines for corporations in violation of Health and Safety regulations. Other changes will take effect in 1991.

Additional information may be obtained from the Occupational Health and Safety Division, Ontario Ministry of Labour, in the following cities:

Toronto
Head Office
400 University Avenue
Toronto, Ontario
M7A 1T7
Tel: (416) 326-7770 - Construction Health and Safety
(416) 326-7900 - Industrial Health and Safety

• District Offices – Industrial Health and Safety Branch

Barrie
114 Worsley Street
5th Floor
Barrie, Ontario
L4M 1M1
Tel: (705) 722-6642
Toll free: 1-800-461-4383

Hamilton
119 King Street West
8th Floor
Hamilton, Ontario
L8N 3Z9
Tel: (416) 521-7736
Toll free: 1-800-263-6906/8

Kingston
1055 Princess Street
Kingston, Ontario
K7L 5T3
Tel: (613) 545-4340
Toll free: 1-800-267-0915

Kitchener
824 King Street West
Kitchener, Ontario
N2G 1G1
Tel: (519) 744-8101
Toll free: 1-800-265-2468/9

London
205 Oxford Street East
2nd Floor
London, Ontario
N6A 5G6
Tel: (519) 439-3231
Toll free: 1-800-265-4707

Mississauga
2 Robert Speck Parkway
3rd Floor
Mississauga, Ontario
L4Z 1H8
Tel: (416) 273-7800
Toll free: 1-800-268-2966/7

North Bay
1500 Fisher Street
2nd Floor
North Bay, Ontario
P1B 2H3
Tel: (705) 476-2711
Toll free: 1-800-461-1654

Ottawa
2197 Riverside Drive
Ottawa, Ontario
K1H 7X3
Tel: (613) 523-7530
Toll free: 1-800-267-1916

Peterborough
815 High Street
Park Lane Plaza
Peterborough, Ontario
K9J 8J9
Tel: (705) 876-1800
Toll free: 1-800-461-1425

Sarnia
700 Christina Street North
Sarnia, Ontario
N7V 3C2
Tel: (519) 336-1200
Toll free: 1-800-265-1416

Sault Ste. Marie
390 Bay Street
3rd Floor
Sault Ste. Marie, Ontario
P6A 1X2
Tel: (705) 949-3331
Toll free: 1-800-416-4000

Scarborough
2500 Lawrence Ave. East
Scarborough, Ontario
M1P 2R7
Tel: (416) 750-3557
Toll free: 1-800-268-6541

St. Catharines
205 King Street
St. Catharines, Ontario
L2R 3J5
Tel: (416) 682-7261
Toll free: 1-800-263-7260

Sudbury
199 Larch Street
Sudbury, Ontario
P3E 5P9
Tel: (705) 675-4455
Toll free: 1-800-461-4000

Thunder Bay
435 James Street South
P.O. Box 5000
Postal Station F
Thunder Bay, Ontario
P7E 6E3
Tel: (807) 475-1691
Toll free: 1-800-465-5016/7

Timmins
Timcor Building
273 Third Avenue
4th Floor
Timmins, Ontario
P4N 1E2
Tel: (705) 267-6231
Toll free: 1-800-461-9847

Windsor
500 Ouellette Avenue
Room 305
Windsor, Ontario
N9A 1B3
Tel: (519) 256-8277
Toll free: 1-800-265-5140/4

• District Offices – Construction Health and Safety Branch:

Hamilton
Ontario Government
Building
105 Main Street East
Suite 807
Hamilton, Ontario
L8N 1G8
Tel: (416) 521-7746
Toll free: 1-800-263-9296

Kingston
1055 Princess Street
Suite 105
Kingston, Ontario
K7L 1H3
Tel: (613) 545-4340
Toll free: 1-800-267-0915

Kitchener
824 King Street West
4th Floor
Kitchener, Ontario
N2G 1G1
Toll free: 1-800-265-2468/9

Kitchener
CHSB Training Unit
195 King Street West
Kitchener, Ontario
N2G 1B1
Tel: (519) 744-7221
Toll free: 1-800-265-2141

London
1020 Hargrieve Road
Main Floor
London, Ontario
N6E 1P7
Tel: (519) 681-1784
Toll free: 1-800-265-7685

Mississauga
2 Robert Speck Parkway
3rd Floor
Mississauga, Ontario
L4Z 1H8
Tel: (416) 273-7800
Toll free: 1-800-268-2966

Ottawa
2197 Riverside Drive
Pebb Bldg., 3rd Floor
Ottawa, Ontario
K1H 7X3
Tel: (613) 523-7530
Toll free: 1-800-267-1916

Peterborough
815 High Street
Park Lane Plaza
Peterborough, Ontario
K9J 8J9
Tel: (705) 876-1800
Toll free: 1-800-461-1425

Sault Ste. Marie
390 Bay Street
3rd Floor
Sault Ste. Marie, Ontario
P6A 1X2
Tel: (705) 949-3331
Toll free: 1-800-461-7268

Scarborough
10 Milner Business Court
Suite 404
Scarborough, Ontario
M1B 3C6
Tel: (416) 609-9467
Toll free: 1-800-268-6541

St. Catharines
205 King Street
Ground Floor
St. Catharines, Ontario
L2R 3J5
Tel: (416) 682-7261
Toll free: 1-800-263-7260

Sudbury
199 Larch Street
6th Floor
Sudbury, Ontario
P3E 5P9
Tel: (705) 675-4455
Toll free: 1-800-461-4000

Thunder Bay
435 James Street South
P.O. Box 5000
Thunder Bay, Ontario
P7E 6E3
Tel: (807) 475-1691
Toll free: 1-800-465-5016/7

Timmins
Timcor Building
4th Floor
273 Third Avenue
Timmins, Ontario
P4N 1E2
Tel: (705) 267-6231
Toll free: 1-800-461-9847

Windsor
500 Ouellette Avenue
Suite 305
Windsor, Ontario
N9A 1B3
Tel: (519) 256-8277
Toll free: 1-800-265-5140/4

- **Ministry of Labour –**
Mining Health and Safety Branch:

Sudbury
Head Office
159 Cedar Street
3rd Floor
Sudbury, Ontario
P3E 6A5
Tel: (705) 670-7400
Toll free: 1-800-461-6325

- **District Offices**

Cable Testing Lab
Room B441, Basement
Whitney Block
Queen's Park
Toronto, Ontario
M7A 1W3
Tel: (416) 965-1327

Elliot Lake
Algo Centre Mall
151 Ontario Avenue
Elliot Lake, Ontario
P5A 2T2
Tel: (705) 848-2885

Kingston
1055 Princess Street
Suite 301
Kingston, Ontario
K7L 1H3
Tel: (613) 545-4335
Toll free: 1-800-267-0915

Kirkland Lake
6 Tweedsmuir Avenue
Kirkland Lake, Ontario
P2N 1H9
Tel: (705) 567-5292

London
1020 Hargrieve Road
London, Ontario
N6E 1P6
Tel: (519) 681-1784
Toll free: 1-800-265-4707

Mine Reserve
Unit 3
674 Notre Dame Avenue
Sudbury, Ontario
P3A 2T7
Tel: (705) 675-4109

Sudbury
199 Larch Street
Provincial Building
6th Floor
Sudbury, Ontario
P3E 5P7
Tel: (705) 675-4464
Toll free: 1-800-461-4000

Technical Support Group
260 Cedar Street
Sudbury, Ontario
P3B 3X2
Tel: (705) 675-4468
Toll free: 1-800-461-4000

Thunder Bay
435 James Street South
P.O. Box 5000
Thunder Bay, Ontario
P7E 6E3
Tel: (807) 475-1691
Toll free: 1-800-465-5016/7

Timmins
Timcor Building
273 Third Avenue
Suite 204
Timmins, Ontario
P4N 1E2
Tel: (705) 267-6231
Toll free: 1-800-461-9847

HEALTH INSURANCE IN ONTARIO

The Ontario Ministry of Health administers a comprehensive government plan of health insurance for Ontario residents. It provides a wide range of benefits for medical and hospital services; additional benefits are also provided for the services of certain other health practitioners.
Residents of Ontario - regardless of age, state of health or financial means - are entitled to participate. Tourists, transients and visitors to Ontario are not eligible.
For further information on any matter concerning health coverage telephone, write or visit your local health insurance office.

• Health Insurance Offices

Barrie
30 Poyntz Street
Barrie, Ontario
L4M 3P2
Tel: (705) 726-0326

Hamilton
119 King Street West
Hamilton, Ontario
L8P 4T9
Tel: (416) 521-7100

Kenora
100 Main Street South
Kenora, Ontario
P9N 1S9
Tel: (807) 468-2869

Kingston
1055 Princess Street
Kingston, Ontario
K7L 5T3
Tel: (613) 546-3811

Kitchener
Canada Life Square
235 King Street East
Kitchener, Ontario
N2G 4N5
Tel: (519) 745-8421

London
227 Queens Avenue
London, Ontario
N6A 1J8
Tel: (519) 433-4561

Mississauga
201 City Centre Drive
Mississauga, Ontario
L5B 2T4
Tel: (416) 275-2730

Oshawa
Executive Tower
Oshawa Centre
419 King Street West
Oshawa, Ontario
L1J 7J2
Tel: (416) 434-3700

Ottawa
75 Albert Street
Ottawa, Ontario
K1P 5Y9
Tel: (613) 783-4400

Owen Sound
981 2nd Avenue East
Owen Sound, Ontario
N4K 2H8
Tel: (519) 376-6447

Peterborough
Park Lane Plaza
815 High Street
Peterborough, Ontario
K9J 8J9
Tel: (705) 743-2140

Sarnia
452 Christina Street North
Sarnia, Ontario
N7T 5W4
Tel: (519) 337-2348

Sault Ste. Marie
205 McNabb Street
Suite 205
Sault Ste. Marie, Ontario
P6B 1Y3
Tel: (705) 759-8598

St. Catharines
59 Church Street
3rd Floor
St. Catharines, Ontario
L2R 3C3
Tel: (416) 682-6658

Sudbury
199 Larch Street
8th Floor
Sudbury, Ontario
P3E 5R1
Tel: (705) 675-4010

Thunder Bay
435 James Street South
Thunder Bay, Ontario
P7E 6E3
Tel: (807) 475-1351

Timmins
38 Pine Street North
101 Mall, Suite 110
Timmins, Ontario
P4N 6K6
Tel: (705) 264-5388

Toronto
2195 Yonge Street
Toronto, Ontario
M4S 2B2
Tel: (416) 482-1111

Toronto
7 Overlea Blvd.
Toronto, Ontario
M4H 1A8
Tel: (416) 965-1000

Windsor
1427 Ouellette Avenue
Windsor, Ontario
N8X 1K1
Tel: (519) 258-7560

EMPLOYER HEALTH TAX

The Ministry of Revenue, Employer Health Tax Branch, administers the Employer Health Tax Act, 1989 which replaced Ontario Health Insurance Plan premiums. The Employer Health Tax (EHT) is payable by all employers paying remuneration to employees who report for work at a permanent establishment in Ontario. It also applies to employers where the employees are not required to report for work at any establishment of the employer when the remuneration is paid from a permanent establishment in Ontario. For further information or assistance call:

> Metro Toronto residents - (416) 965-8470
> All other Ontario residents - 1-800-263-7965
> Users of a Telecommunications
> Device for the Deaf - 1-800-263-7776

Or write to:

> Ministry of Revenue
> Employer Health Tax
> P.O. Box 627
> 33 King Street West
> Oshawa, Ontario
> L1H 8H5

CHAPTER 9:
SOURCES OF INFORMATION

The Ministry of Industry, Trade and Technology provides

counselling and assistance programs to small businesses

through a network of province-wide offices and associated

agencies. These offices provide initial and continuing con-

tact for small business assistance. Local services are sup-

plemented by seminars scheduled throughout Ontario and

self-help publications available by mail order or at a grow-

ing number of local outlets.

**MINISTRY OF
INDUSTRY, TRADE
AND TECHNOLOGY
SERVICES**

The Small Business Start-up Hotline
    The Ministry's Small Business Start-up Hotline provides toll-free information on Provincial services and the rules and regulations affecting those wishing to start their own business. The Hotline operates from 8:00 a.m. to 5:00 p.m., Monday to Friday at 1-800-567-2345 or in the Toronto area call (416) 963-0050.

Seminars
    The Ministry of Industry, Trade and Technology offers seminars on Starting a Small Business in Ontario. Seminars present information on business start-ups and also provide a forum for questions and answers. In addition, seminars are given on marketing and franchising. There is a nominal fee for these seminars.
    For further information on small business seminars contact the Small Business Start-up Hotline at 1-800-567-2345 or in the Toronto area call (416) 963-0050.

Publications

The Ministry has established a series of self-help small business publications to support business development. In addition to "Starting a Small Business in Ontario" there are several workbooks which have been developed for the service, retail and manufacturing sectors. Each workbook covers theory, examples of putting the theory into practice and blank forms for your use. Topics include: How to Prepare a Business Plan and Marketing.

The "Record Keeping Made Easy" publication will help businesses establish an easy-to-use cash management and recordkeeping system and contains all that is needed to maintain a full set of records for one year.

These publications may be purchased for a nominal fee from your nearest Business Self-Help Office or from Publications Ontario. To order by mail or telephone use the tear-out mail order card included in this book.

Business Self-Help Offices

Business self-help offices offer information and advice to anyone wanting to start their own business. Each office is a one-step, first stop source of information with access to resource materials and personal advice on preparing a business plan, managing a new business and government assistance to entrepreneurs.

• Southern Ontario

Brantford Business Self-Help Office
City Hall
100 Wellington Square
Brantford, Ontario
N3T 2M3
Tel: (519) 759-4150
Ext. 256
Fax: (519) 752-6775

Hamilton-Wentworth Business Advisory Centre
1 James Street South
P.O. Box 910
7th Floor
Hamilton, Ontario
L8N 3V9
Tel: (416) 577-6606
Fax: (416) 528-8725

Huntsville Business Self-Help Office
8 West Street North
Huntsville, Ontario
P0A 1K0
Tel: (705) 789-6693
Fax: (705) 789-6689

Kitchener Business Self-Help Office
22 Frederick Street
6th Floor
Kitchener, Ontario
N2G 4G7
Tel: (519) 741-2604
Fax: (519) 741-2222

London Business Self-Help Office
1764 Oxford Street East
London, Ontario
N5V 3R6
Tel: (519) 659-1882
Fax: (519) 451-7889

Markham Business Self-Help Office
Scotiabank Commercial
Tower
625 Cochrane Drive
Suite 903
Markham, Ontario
L3R 9R9
Tel: (416) 475-4890
Fax: (416) 474-0685

Newcomers Business Self-Help Office
Kensington Campus
George Brown College
21 Nassau Street
Toronto, Ontario
M5T 1M3
Tel: (416) 867-2370
Fax: (416) 867-2371

Peel Business Self-Help Office
4 Robert Speck Parkway
11th Floor
Mississauga, Ontario
L4Z 1S1
Tel: (416) 279-6515
Fax: (416) 279-9160

Queen's Park Business Self-Help Office
900 Bay Street
7th Floor
Toronto, Ontario
M7A 2E1
Tel: (416) 965-5494
Fax: (416) 324-6987

Scarborough Business Self-Help Office
150 Borough Drive
Scarborough, Ontario
M1P 4N7
Tel: (416) 396-7169
Fax: (416) 396-4241

Toronto Business Self-Help Office
Main Floor – City Hall
Toronto, Ontario
M5H 2N2
Tel: (416) 392-6646
Fax: (416) 392-0797

Windsor Business Self-Help Office
Ontario Government
Building
250 Windsor Avenue
Room 227
Windsor, Ontario
N9A 6V9
Tel: (519) 252-3475 or
1-800-265-1345
Fax: (519) 252-9677

• Eastern Ontario

**Kingston Business
Self-Help Office**
275 Ontario Street,
Suite 100
Kingston, Ontario
K7K 2X5
Tel: (613) 544-2725
Fax: (613) 546-2882

**Hastings Business
Self-Help Office**
5 Stewart Street
Trenton, Ontario
K8V 6H5
Tel: (613) 394-6616
Fax: (613) 394-5976

**Hawkesbury Business
Self-Help Office**
600 Higginson Street
Hawkesbury, Ontario
K6A 1H1
Tel: (613) 632-7057
Fax: (613) 632-8694

**Northumberland
Business Self-Help Office**
The Fleming Building
1005 William Street, Suite 202
Cobourg, Ontario
K9A 5J4
Tel: (416) 372-9279
Fax: (416) 372-1306

**Ottawa Business
Self-Help Office**
Place de Ville – Tower B
112 Kent Street, Suite 870
Ottawa, Ontario
K1P 5P2
Tel: (613) 566-3703
Fax: (613) 563-0436

**Peterborough Business
Self-Help Office**
City Hall
500 George Street North
Peterborough, Ontario
K9H 3R9
Tel: (705) 876-4602
Fax: (705) 742-5218

**Renfrew Business
Self-Help Office**
210 Lochiel Street South
P. O. Box 160
Renfrew, Ontario
K7V 4A3
Tel: (613) 432-6848
Fax: (613) 432-8514

**Smiths Falls Business
Self-Help Office**
77 Beckwith Street North
Smiths Falls, Ontario
K7A 2B8
Tel: (613) 283-4124
Fax: (613) 283-1253

• Northern Ontario

**Sault Ste. Marie
Business Self-Help Office**
500 Bay Street
2nd Floor
Sault Ste. Marie, Ontario
P6A 1X4
Tel: (705) 945-8300
Fax: (705) 942-2823

**Sudbury (SRDC)
Business Self-Help Office**
Civic Square – West Tower
200 Brady Street
Sudbury, Ontario
P3E 5K3
Tel: (705) 673-9604
Fax: (705) 671-6767

**Timmins Business
Self-Help Office**
273 Third Avenue
Suite 103
Timmins, Ontario
P4N 1E2
Tel: (705) 264-3400
Fax: (705) 360-1394

**Thunder Bay Business
Self-Help Office**
Ontario Government
Building
435 James Street South
P. O. Box 5000
Thunder Bay, Ontario
P7C 5G6
Tel: (807) 475-1647
Fax: (807) 475-1665

**Timiskaming Business
Self-Help Office**
95 Meridian Avenue
Haileybury, Ontario
P0J 1K0
Tel: (705) 672-5155
Fax: (705) 672-5466

**North Bay Business
Self-Help Office**
200 McIntyre Street East
P. O. Box 360
North Bay, Ontario
P1B 8H8
Tel: (705) 474-0400
Fax: (705) 474-4493

There are 18 Ministry of Industry, Trade and Technology field offices in Ontario.

• Central-East Ontario
Area office in Metro Toronto (Fairview Mall)
District office in Orillia

Metro Toronto
5 Fairview Mall Drive
Suite 480
Willowdale, Ontario
M2J 2Z1
Tel: (416) 491-7680

Orillia
General Trust Building
73 Mississaga Street East
2nd Floor
P.O.Box 488
Orillia, Ontario
L3V 6K2
Tel: (705) 325-1363

Eastern Ontario
Area office in Ottawa
District offices in Kingston and Peterborough

Kingston
1055 Princess Street
Suite 308
Kingston, Ontario
K7L 5T3
Tel: (613) 545-4444

Peterborough
139 George Street North
Peterborough, Ontario
K9J 3G6
Tel: (705) 742-3459

Ottawa
Place de Ville, Tower B
Suite 870
112 Kent Street
Ottawa, Ontario
K1P 5P2
Tel: (613) 566-3703

• Central-West Ontario
Area office in Hamilton
District offices in St. Catharines and Peel

Hamilton
Bank of Montreal Tower
1 James Street North
Suite 200
Hamilton, Ontario
L8R 2K3
Tel: (416) 521-7783

St. Catharines
Suite 801
80 King Street
Corbloc Building
St. Catharines, Ontario
L2R 7G1
Tel: (416) 688-1454

Peel
11th Floor
4 Robert Speck Parkway
Mississauga, Ontario
L4Z 1S1
Tel: (416) 279-6515

• Northern Ontario
Area office in Sault Ste. Marie
District offices in Timmins, Thunder Bay, North Bay and Sudbury

North Bay
147 McIntyre Street West
North Bay, Ontario
P1B 2Y5
Tel: (705) 472-9660

Thunder Bay
Ontario Government
Building
435 James Street South
3rd Floor
P.O. Box 5000
Thunder Bay, Ontario
P7C 5G6
Tel: (807) 475-4088

Sault Ste. Marie
500 Bay Street
Box 1196
Sault Ste. Marie, Ontario
P6A 1X4
Tel: (705) 945-8300

Timmins
273 Third Avenue
Suite 200
Timmins, Ontario
P4N 1E2
(705) 264-5393

Sudbury
Ontario Government
Building
199 Larch Street
4th Floor
Sudbury, Ontario
P3E 5P9
Tel: (705) 675-4330

• Southwestern Ontario

Area office in London
District office in Windsor, Kitchener, Owen Sound
and Sarnia

Kitchener
30 Duke Street West
Suite 906
Kitchener, Ontario
N2H 3W5
Tel: (519) 744-6391

London
195 Dufferin Avenue
Suite 607
London, Ontario
N6A 1K7
Tel: (519) 433-8105

Owen Sound
1137 Second Avenue East
Owen Sound, Ontario
N4K 2J1
Tel: (519) 376-3875
Toll free in (519) area code
only 1-800-265-3796

Sarnia
201 Front Street North
Suite 801
Sarnia, Ontario
N7T 7T9
Tel: (519) 332-5030

Windsor
Ontario Government
Building
250 Windsor Avenue
Room 227
Windsor, Ontario
N9A 6V9
Tel: (519) 252-3475

Ontario Ministry of Industry, Trade and Technology international offices are gateways to the major industrial and trading centres of the world for Ontario business people. They are also the first point of contact for international business people seeking contact with the Province of Ontario.

International officers provide an array of services concerning industrial development and export marketing. As well, they are ready to assist business people looking for manufacturing and licensing arrangements, opportunities for industrial investment and marketing assistance.

• United States

Atlanta, Georgia
Government of Ontario
(Canada)
Suite 620
1100 Circle
75 Parkway
Atlanta, Georgia
30339
Tel: (404) 956-1981

Boston, Massachusetts
Government of Ontario
(Canada)
Suite 4360
Prudential Center
800 Boylston Street
Boston, Massachusetts
02199-8001

Los Angeles, California
Government of Ontario
(Canada)
Suite 1420
700 South Flower Street
Los Angeles, California
Tel: (617) 266-7172

Chicago, Illinois
Government of Ontario
(Canada)
Suite 2700
221 North LaSalle Street
Chicago, Illinois
60601
Tel: (312) 782-8688

Dallas, Texas
Government of Ontario
(Canada)
Suite 485
14901 Quorum Drive
Dallas, Texas
75240
Tel: (214) 386-8071

New York, New York
Government of Ontario
(Canada)
Suite 2800
800 Third Avenue
New York, New York
10022
Tel: (212) 308-1616

• Europe

Frankfurt, Germany
Government of Ontario/
Canada
Bockenheimer
Landstr. 51-53
D-6000 Frankfurt/Main
Germany
Tel: 011-49-69-71-91990
Fax: 011-49-69-71-9199-28

London, England
Government of Ontario/
Canada
21 Knightsbridge
SW1X 7LY, London
England
Tel: 011-44-71-245-1222
Fax: 011-44-71-259-6661

Milan, Italy
Delegation of
Ontario/Canada
Piazza della Repubblica, 12
Piano 2
20124 Milan, Italy
Tel: 011-39-2-659-2255
or 011-39-2-659-2028
Fax: 011-39-2-2317

Paris, France
Delegation of Ontario/
Canada
109, rue du Faubourg
St-Honoré
Paris 75008, France
Tel: 011-33-1-4563-1634
Fax: 011-33-1-4-225-3839

Stuttgart, Germany
Government of
Ontario/Canada
Charlottenplatz 17
7000 Stuttgart 1
Germany
Tel: 011-49-711-226-19-91
Fax: 011-49-711-226-88-68

• Pacific Rim

Hong Kong
Government of Ontario
(Canada)
Room 906-908
Hutchison House
10 Harcourt Road
Hong Kong
Tel: 5-8453388

New Delhi
Government of
Ontario/Canada
17 Jor Bagh, Lodi Road
New Delhi 110-003
India
Tel: 011-91-11-624-603
Fax: 011-91-11-462-5333

Seoul
Ontario Representative
Canadian Embassy
10th Floor, Kolon Building
45 Mugyo-Dong, Jung-Ku
P.O. Box 6299
Seoul 100, Korea
Tel: 011-82-2-753-2605

Singapore
Government of Ontario
(Canada)
Office of the Agent of
Ontario
Liat Tower
541 Orchard Road
Suite 1003
Singapore
Tel: 011-65-732-4567

Tokyo, Japan
Government of Ontario
(Canada)
World Trade Centre
Building, R1219
4-1 Hamamatsu-Cho
2 Chome, Minato-Ku
Tokyo 105, Japan
Tel: 011-81-3-436-4355

FEDERAL ASSISTANCE PROGRAMS

Business Service Centre
Communications Branch
Department of Industry,
Science and Technology
Canada
1 Front Street West
4th Floor
Dominion Public Building
Toronto, Ontario
M5J 1A4
Tel: (416) 973-4782

Provides information and counselling on programs and services offered specifically by ISTC.

District Offices:
Northeastern (Sudbury)
Tel: (705) 671-0711
Northwestern (Thunder
Bay)
Tel: (807) 623-4436

119

Following is a list of associations that can help your business venture in many ways. Some can help you with information and guidance, others by providing you with a voice for your industry or an opportunity to meet your customers and keep a high profile.

Check your telephone book for other local business associations, city-based associations and area associations.

GENERAL BUSINESS
ASSOCIATIONS

Canadian Franchise Association
88 University Avenue
Suite 607
Toronto, Ontario
M5J 1T6

Holds seminars and lunches. Provides services to member franchisors. Restricted to services for members only.

Canadian Association for Home-Based Business
1200E Prince of Wales Drive
Ottawa, Ontario
K2C 1M9
Tel: (613) 723-7233

A national association for home-based businesses which produces newsletters, directories and other resource material. Hosts conferences and a variety of events in support of the self-employed small business person.

Canadian Association of Family Enterprise
615 Yonge Street
5th Floor
Toronto, Ontario
M4Y 2T4
Tel: (416) 966-0661

Local chapter meetings. Networks and assists members with passing on business, training heirs and dealing with other issues.

Canadian Centre for Occupational Health and Safety
250 Main Street East
Hamilton, Ontario
L8N 1H6
Tel: (416) 572-2981

The centre provides occupational health and safety information through responses to inquiries, publications and a computerized information service.

120

The Canadian Chamber of Commerce
120 Adelaide Street West
Suite 2109
Toronto, Ontario
M5H 1T1
Tel: (416) 868-6415

Has a small business committee, an active body lobbying on the federal government level. Co-sponsor of Small Business Week. Membership fee, a minimum of $150 per year, entitles the member to copies of Ottawa Update, reflecting current federal legislation, and copies of "Impact", discussing Chamber activities.

Canadian Council of Better Business Bureaus
2180 Steeles Avenue West
Suite 219
Concord, Ontario
L4K 2Z5
Tel: (416) 669-1248

Businesses may join national or local division only. Co-ordinates 17 offices across Canada. Local divisions assist businesses with various services. Membership not required to receive information or assistance.

Canadian Direct Marketing Association
1 Concord Gate
Suite 607
Don Mills, Ontario
M3C 3N6
Tel: (416) 391-2362

No local chapters. Represents the direct marketing industry. Membership compulsory. Fees range from $250 up.

Canadian Federation of Independent Business (CFIB)
4141 Yonge Street
Suite 401
Willowdale, Ontario
M2P 2A6
Tel: (416) 222-8022

Has no local chapters. A political action group for small and medium-sized business in Canada. Services and library mainly for members only. Fees from $75 to $1000 per year.

Canadian Organization of Small Business
Toronto Office
150 Consumers Road
Suite 501
Willowdale, Ontario
M2J 1P9
Tel: (416) 492-3223

Head office in Edmonton. Represents independent business by lobbying government. Services for members only. Fees from $150.

Canadian Standards Association
178 Rexdale Blvd.
Rexdale, Ontario
M9W 1R3
Tel: (416) 747-4000

Has volunteer and corporate members. Provides Canadian standards and related services for the benefit of the public, government and business. Services available to all.

Direct Sellers Association
4950 Yonge Street
Suite 1400
North York, Ontario
M2N 6K1
Tel: (416) 733-8071

No local chapters. Represents the direct selling (but not direct mail) industry in Canada. Services are for members but will try to help callers. New businesses should call their lawyers due to legal complexities surrounding direct selling.

Ontario Chamber of Commerce
2323 Yonge Street
5th Floor
Toronto, Ontario
M4P 2C9
Tel: (416) 482-5222

Local chambers. Lobby group for business in Ontario represented by 150 local chambers. Services for members only. Sponsorship not required for membership.

Ontario Crafts Council
35 McCaul Street
Toronto, Ontario
M5T 1V7
Tel: (416) 977-3551

Offers counselling to craftspeople on going into business. Monthly and quarterly bulletins and magazines for a $25 yearly membership fee. Monthly shows in craft gallery.

Small Business Network
2180 Steeles Avenue West
Suite 217
Concord, Ontario
L4K 2Z5
Tel: (416) 221-8040

Monthly meetings. Assists small business owners to make contacts and get started in business. Services for members.

CONSULTING
INDUSTRY

Canadian Association of Management Consultants
121 Bloor Street East
Suite 805
Toronto, Ontario
M4W 3M5
Tel: (416) 963-9172

Has no local chapters. Is a trade association representing member Canadian consulting firms.

FOOD AND BEVERAGE
INDUSTRY

Canadian Specialty Food Association
1 Eva Road
Suite 409
Etobicoke, Ontario
M9C 4Z5
Tel: (416) 626-6239

No local chapters. Trade association representing manufacturers, retailers, importers, distributors, brokers. Bi-monthly newsletter and group discounts for members. Educational seminars and annual trade show open to non-members.

Ontario Restaurant Association
121 Richmond Street West
Suite 638
Toronto, Ontario
M5H 2K1
Tel: (416) 359-0533

Has regional divisions. Responsible for government liaison, mailing lists and guides to suppliers for members. Services for members only.

MANUFACTURING
INDUSTRY

Canadian Manufacturers' Association
1 Yonge Street
Suite 1400
Toronto, Ontario
M5E 1J9
Tel: (416) 363-7261

Seminars held throughout the province. CMA helps manufacturers run their business better. Only manufacturers can be members.

**Accommodation Motel
Ontario Association**
1837 Lansdowne Street
West
Unit 4A
Peterborough, Ontario
K9K 1R4
Tel: (705) 745-4982

*No local chapters. Local
motel associations are not
affiliated with this association. The association represents members to govern-
ment, promotes the industry
and furthers member growth.
Members must offer
overnight accommodation
under Ontario legislation.*

**Ontario Private
Campground
Association**
55 Nugget Avenue
Suite 230
Scarborough, Ontario
M1S 3L1
Tel: (416) 293-2090

*No local chapters. Regional
directors hold their own
meetings. The association
promotes the industry and
works to make it more viable
in the province. Services not
restricted to members. Some
data released to members
only.*

Retail Council of Canada
210 Dundas Street West
Suite 600
Toronto, Ontario
M5G 2E8
Tel: (416) 598-4684

*Members get involved
through committee work. The
council represents the retail
community to government.
Services to members only.*

**Retail Merchants
Association of Canada
(Ont.) Inc.**
1780 Birchmount Road
Scarborough, Ontario
M1P 2H8
Tel: (416) 291-7903

*No local chapters. This is an
organization for small independent retailers and provides services such as bulk
buying and coupon counting.
Services for members only.*

**Canadian Export
Association**
99 Bank Street
Suite 250
Ottawa, Ontario
K1P 6B9
Tel: (613) 238-8888

*Promotes exporters and
exporting in Canada. Some
publications are for members
only.*

**Canadian Importers
Association**
210 Dundas Street West
Suite 700
Toronto, Ontario
M5G 2E8
Tel: (416) 595-5333

*Has committees through
which members can become
involved. For importing, the
association helps with trou-
bleshooting and problem
solving. You must be a member. For new importers,
"Import Canada" Seminars
are offered.*

General business associations for women in business

**Canadian Association of
Women
Executives &
Entrepreneurs**
1980 Queen Street East
2nd Floor
Toronto, Ontario
M4L 1J2
Tel: (416) 690-5142

*Frequent meetings but most
held in Toronto. Chapters
elsewhere planned for the
future. Members are business
owners and executives in corporations. Services are not
restricted to members.*

**Canadian Association of
Women
Business Owners**
2007 The Chase
Mississauga, Ontario
L5M 2W2
Tel: (416) 820-9206

*For women in business for
themselves, particularly in
the service sector. Also a self-
help group. Encourages
women to run profitable and
non-traditional business.
Services are for members
only.*

Canadian Federation of Business and Professional Women's Clubs
56 Sparks Street
Suite 308
Ottawa, Ontario
K1P 5A9
Tel: (613) 234-7619

Has local chapters in many Ontario cities, including Brampton, Cobourg, Dryden, Kingston, Ottawa, Toronto. Promotes equality of women in the workplace. Sponsorship not required.

Women's Initiatives for Successful Entrepreneurship
(Southwestern Ontario)
79 Ridout Street South
London, Ontario
N6C 3X2
Tel: (519) 679-2470

Provides information, education and non-financial support to women business owners and women contemplating ownership. Holds workshops, conferences and seminars.

Women Entrepreneurs Committee, Sudbury Business and Professional Women's Club
P.O. Box 2593 Station A
Sudbury, Ontario
P3A 4S9
Tel: (705) 566-8101

Promotes and encourages women to pursue and engage in business ownership. Services not restricted to members.

Women Business Owners Organization of Northwestern Ontario
c/o Northwest Enterprise Centre
P.O. Box 398
Thunder Bay, Ontario
P7C 4W1
Tel: (807) 475-6400
1-800-465-6961, Ext. 400

For potential and established women business owners/operators. Provides direction, information sources, seminars, workshops and networking forums.

The Limestone Club
174 Division Street
Kingston, Ontario
K7L 3B8

Club members are looking to broaden their horizons through personal profession-al growth. A forum where they can expand their net-work of business contacts.

Women on the Move
Algoma Networking, Inc.
P.O. Box 1375
Sault Ste. Marie, Ontario
P6N 6N2

Promotes and encourages women to pursue and engage in business ownership. Provides direction, informa-tion sources and networking forums.

These associations are either specific industry-focussed or act as networks for women to meet. To find out if there is one in your town or city check the white pages and yellow pages or ask for referrals to such groups.

The Women's Advertising Club of Toronto
1 Yonge Street
Suite 1801
Toronto, Ontario
M5E 1W7

Hamilton-Wentworh Women's Connection
c/o Hamilton Status of Women Committee
City Hall, Main Street West
Hamilton, Ontario
L8N 3T4
Tel: (416) 546-3993

Women in Trades
c/o Times Change
22 Davisville Avenue
Toronto, Ontario
M4S 1E8

Women's Economic Forum
1361 Ouellette Avenue
Windsor, Ontario
M8X 1J7
Tel: (519) 252-4234

Third Thursday Network

Mövenpick Restaurant
165 York Street
Toronto, Ontario
M5H 3R8
Tel: (416) 366-5234

Canada Jaycees
39 Leacock Way
Kanata, Ontario
K2K 1T1
Tel: (613) 592-2450

Leadership training organization with local chapters in different cities. Open to those 18 to 40.

Junior Achievement of Canada
75 Browns Line
Toronto, Ontario
M8W 3S2
Tel: (416) 252-4602
Toronto Chapter
Tel: (416) 977-6000

The purpose of Junior Achievement is to promote economic literacy and understanding of business and private enterprise among Canadian youth.

Ministry of Skills Development
5th Floor
625 Church Street
Toronto, Ontario
M4Y 2E8
Tel: (416) 326-5605

Administers a number of youth employment initiatives. The Ministry also provides counselling services and publications to help youth secure employment.

The YMCA of Metropolitan Toronto
Youth Enterprise
Toronto, Ontario
M6C 3Y4
Tel: (416) 651-0010

Provides free consulting, training and support to young entrepreneurs (under the age of 30 and not employed or in school on a full time basis) who are planning the start of their own business.

Ottawa YM-YWCA
Youth Enterprise
1550 Carling Avenue
Ottawa, Ontario
K1Z 7P8
Tel: (613) 728-6925

CHAPTER 10:
BIBLIOGRAPHY

There are many books that provide insight and knowledge

for the new businessperson. These are recent publications;

several have been written by entrepreneurs like yourself.

Try your local public library; if these books are not

available they may be able to search and reserve them for

you through the public library system.

• Advertising, Promotion and Public Relations

The Ad Game: Recreating Creativity .. to Sell
Robert Cohen
CCH Canadian Limited, 1987
ISBN 0-88796-409-5

The Advertising Handbook: Make a Big Impact with a Small Business Budget
Dell Dennison and Linda Tobey
Self-Counsel Press, 1991
ISBN 0-88908-954-X

• Franchising

Franchising: A Complete Guide for Canadian Buyers and Sellers
Bev Cline
Key Porter Books, 1989
ISBN 1-55013-113-3

Franchising in Canada: Pros and Cons
Michael M. Coltman
Self-Counsel Press, 2nd Edition, 1987
ISBN 0-88908-667-2

**Franchising in Canada:
A Guide for Franchisors
and Franchisees,
Business, Taxation and
Accounting Issues**
Taylor Gilbert, David
Thomson and Peter
Dabbikeh
CCH Canadian Limited,
1986
ISBN 0-88796-345-5

• General

**Buying and Selling a
Small Business in
Canada**
Michael M. Coltman
Self-Counsel Press, 2nd
Edition - 1989
ISBN 0-88908-694-X

**The Canadian Small
Business Guide**
Vivienne Monty
CCH Canadian Limited,
1985
ISBN 0-88796-285-8

**The Complete Canadian
Small Business Guide**
Douglas A. Gray and Diana
Lynn Gray
McGraw-Hill Ryerson, 1988
ISBN 0-07-549595-3

**Federal Incorporation
and Business Guide**
M. Stephen Georgas, LL.B.
Self-Counsel Press, 7th
Edition - 1991
ISBN 0-88908-961-2

Growing a Business
Paul Hawken
Collins Publishers, 1987
ISBN 0-00-217903-2

**Incorporation and
Business Guide for
Ontario**
M. Stephen Georgas, LL.B.
Self-Counsel Press,
10th Edition - 1989
ISBN 0-88908-374-6

**Small Business Success:
A Practical Guide for the
Entrepreneur**
Tony Fattal
CCH Canadian Limited,
1989
ISBN 0-88796-526-1

• Special-Focus Books

Home Inc.: The Canadian Home-Based Business Guide
Douglas A. Gray & Diana Lynn Gray
McGraw-Hill Ryerson Limited, 1989
ISBN 0-07-549872-3

Start and Run a Profitable Consulting Business
Douglas A. Gray
Self-Counsel Press, 3rd Edition - August 1990
ISBN 0-88908-897-7

Start and Run a Profitable Craft Business
William G. Hynes
Self-Counsel Press, 3rd Edition - March 1990
ISBN 0-88908-883-7

Start and Run a Profitable Home-Based Business
Edna Sheedy
Self-Counsel Press, 1990
ISBN 0-88908-877-2

Start and Run a Profitable Restaurant: A Step-by-Step Business Plan
Michael M. Coltman
Self-Counsel Press, 2nd Edition - February 1991
ISBN 0-88908-953-1

Start and Run a Profitable Retail Business
Michael M. Coltman
Self-Counsel Press, 2nd Edition - January 1989
ISBN 0-88908-852-7

Selling Strategies for Service Businesses: How to Sell What You Can't See, Taste, or Touch
Karen Johnston and Jean Withers
Self-Counsel Press, 1988
ISBN 0-88908-685-0

• Starting and Managing a Business

A Small Business Guide to Employee Selection: Finding, Interviewing, and Hiring the Right People
Lin Grensing
Self-Counsel Press, 1991
ISBN 0-88908-959-0

The Art and Science of Small Business Management
Gerry S. White
Penguin Books Canada Ltd., 1989
ISBN 0-14-009932-8

Basic Accounting For the Small Business: Simple, Foolproof Techniques For Keeping Your Books Straight and Staying out of Trouble
Clive G. Cornish
Self-Counsel Press, 8th Edition - 1990
ISBN 0-88908-896-9

Be an Even Better Manager: Improve Performance, Profits and Productivity
Michael Armstrong
Self-Counsel Press, 2nd Edition - 1990
ISBN 0-88908-874-8

Buy Yourself a Job & Be Your Own Boss
Graham Cunningham
McGraw-Hill Ryerson Limited, 1990
ISBN 0-07-551057-X

Employee/Employer Rights: A Guide for the Ontario Work Force
Ernest Rovet and Stephen Bernofsky
Self-Counsel Press, 8th Edition - 1990
ISBN 0-88908-378-9

The Entrepreneur's Complete Self-Assessment Guide: How to Accurately Determine Your Potential for Success
Douglas A. Gray
Self-Counsel Press, 2nd Edition - 1990
ISBN 0-88908-878-0

Keeping Customers Happy: Strategies for Success
Jacqueline Dunkel and Brian Taylor
Self-Counsel Press, 2nd Edition - 1990
ISBN 0-88908-887-X

Marketing Your Product: A Planning Guide for Small Business
Douglas A. Gray and Donald Cyr
Self-Counsel Press, 1987
ISBN 0-88908-659-1

Marketing Your Service: A Planning Guide for Small Business
Jean Withers and Carol Vipperman
Self-Counsel Press, 1987
ISBN 0-88908-654-0

Motivating Today's Workforce: When the Carrot Can't Always Be Cash
Lin Grensing
Self-Counsel Press, 1991
ISBN 0-88908-955-8

Preparing a Successful Business Plan: A Practical Guide for Small Business
Rodger D. Touchie
Self-Counsel Press, 1989
ISBN 0-88908-860-8

Standard Legal Forms and Agreements for Canadian Business
Steve Sanderson
Self-Counsel Press, 1989
ISBN 0-88908-865-9

Start Your Own Business: The Canadian Entrepreneur's Guide
Peter D. Cook
Stoddart Publishing Co. Limited, 1989
ISBN 0-7737-5309-5

Starting a Business: A Complete Guide to Starting and Managing Your Own Company
Gordon Brockhouse
Key Porter Books Limited, 1989
ISBN 1-55013-148-6

• Success Stories

Money Makers! The Secrets of Canada's Most Successful Entrepreneurs
Kenneth Barnes and Everett Banning
McClelland and Stewart Limited, 1985
ISBN 0-7710-1047-8

Starting a Successful Business in Canada
Jack D. James
Self-Counsel Press, 10th Edition - 1989
ISBN 0-88908-855-1

Understanding Financial Information: The Non-Financial Manager's Guide
Michael Coltman
Self-Counsel Press, 2nd Edition - 1990
ISBN 0-88908-898-5

Venture Capital in Canada: A Guide and Sources
Industry, Science & Technology Canada and the Association of Canadian Venture Capital Companies
ISBN 0-662-17212-4

The New Entrepreneurs: 80 Canadian Success Stories
Allan Gould
McClelland and Stewart-Bantam Limited, 1986
ISBN 0-7704-2092-3

• Women

**Changing the Rules:
The Woman's Guide to
Starting a Successful
Business**
Marina Mirabella
Stoddart Publishing Co.
Limited, 1988
ISBN 0-7737-5190-4

**Women Mean Business:
Successful Strategies for
Starting your own
Business**
Moneca Litton
Key Porter Books Limited,
1987
ISBN 1-55013-017-X

**Women Like Me: The
Small Business and
Networking Director
(8th National Edition,
1990)**
Karen Fraser
Welcom Limited
ISBN 0-9691274-5-6

• Keeping Up To Date
Even when your business is up and running, it's important to keep on top of trends and have access to the latest ideas. Subscribe to magazines and newsletters tailored to small business. Here are some to consider.

Challenges: Ontario's
Business: Issues and
Opportunities
Ontario Ministry of
Industry, Trade and
Technology
Hearst Block
900 Bay Street
Toronto, Ontario
M7A 2E1

INC.
United Marine Publishing,
Inc.
Box 800, Whitinsville
MA, 01588

Profit: The Magazine for
Canadian Entrepreneurs
CB Media Ltd.
56 The Esplanade
Suite 208
Toronto, Ontario
M5E 1A7

Canadian Business
C.B. Media Ltd.
2nd Floor
70 The Esplanade
Toronto, Ontario
M5E 1R2

Venture: The Magazine for
Entrepreneurs
P.O. Box 10771,
Des Moines, Iowa
50349

Entrepreneur
Chase Revel Inc.
2311 Pontius Avenue
Los Angeles, CA. 90064

• Starting A Business
Here is a partial listing of booklets available for small business.

Bank of Montreal: Has a series of booklets, **Business Problem Solvers**

Canadian Imperial Bank of Commerce: Has book **Doing Business in Canada** and other material.

Canadian Book of Corporate Management
Dun & Bradstreet, annual. Lists top companies and their officers.

Canadian Footwear & Leather Directory,
49th ed.
Lloyd's, 1983

Canadian Furniture & Furnishings Directory
Lloyd's, 1983

Federal Business Development Bank: Has a series of books, **Minding Your Own Business.**

Royal Bank: Provides series **Your Business Matters.**

Canadian Jewellery & Giftware Directory
Lloyd's, 1983

Canadian Sporting Goods & Playthings
Directory
Lloyd's, 1983

Canadian Textile Directory
Sentinel Business Publications, annual.

Canadian Key Business Directory
2 vols.
Dun & Bradstreet, annual
Lists major companies, their earnings, etc.

Directory of Associations in Canada, Annual Micromedia.

Financial Post Survey of Industrials
Maclean-Hunter, annual.

Fraser's Canadian Trade Directory
Maclean-Hunter, annual.

Made in Ontario
Directory of manufacturers,
Ministry of Industry, Trade
and Technology, annual

Million Dollar Directory,
3 vols.
Dun & Bradstreet, annual
All major U.S. and some
Canadian corporations.

Pulp and Paper Canada,
Annual and Directory
Southam Business
Publications, annual.

Scott's Industrial Directories:
Ontario Manufacturers
Scott's Directories, annual.

Directory of Retail Chains in Canada
Maclean-Hunter, annual

Export Canada: The
Marketing Directory for
Canadian Trade Can Expo
Publishers Inc., 1983.

Financial Post Survey of Mines
Maclean-Hunter, annual.

Guide to Canadian Manufacturers
Dun & Bradstreet, annual

Directory of Shopping Centres
in the U.S. & Canada,
annual.

Standard and Poor's Register of Corporations, Directors and Executives, 3 vols.
Standard and Poor's,
annual. All major U.S. and
some Canadian corportions.

Thomas Register of American Manufacturers
Thomas, annual.

INDEX